DATE DU

MALE/FEMALE

ROLES

OPPOSING VIEWPOINTS®

Other Books of Related Interest

Opposing Viewpoints Series

Discrimination
The Family
Feminism
Homosexuality
Human Nature
Human Sexuality
Inequality: Opposing Viewpoints in Social Problems
Pornography
Sexual Values
Sexual Violence
Teenage Pregnancy
Teenage Sexuality
Working Women

Current Controversies Series

Family Violence
Gay Rights
Marriage and Divorce
Sexual Harassment
Violence Against Women

At Issue Series

Affirmative Action
Date Rape
Domestic Violence
Gay Marriage
Rape on Campus
Sex Education
Single-Parent Families
What Is Sexual Harassment?

MALE/FEMALE
ROLES
OPPOSING VIEWPOINTS®

Laura K. Egendorf, Book Editor

David L. Bender, *Publisher*
Bruno Leone, *Executive Editor*
Bonnie Szumski, *Editorial Director*
David M. Haugen, *Managing Editor*

OPPOSING
VIEWPOINTS®
SERIES

Greenhaven Press, Inc., San Diego, California

Cover photo: Planet Art

Library of Congress Cataloging-in-Publication Data

Male/female roles : opposing viewpoints / Laura K. Egendorf, book
    editor.
        p.   cm. — (Opposing viewpoints series)
    Includes bibliographical references and index.
    ISBN 0-7377-0130-7 (pbk. : alk. paper). —
ISBN 0-7377-0131-5 (lib. : alk. paper)
    1. Sex role. 2. Sex role—United States. I. Egendorf, Laura K.,
1973–   . II. Series: Opposing viewpoints series (Unnumbered)
HQ1075.M353 2000
305.3—dc21   99-25743
                                                                   CIP

Greenhaven Press, Inc., P.O. Box 289009
San Diego, CA 92198-9009

"CONGRESS SHALL MAKE NO LAW...ABRIDGING THE FREEDOM OF SPEECH, OR OF THE PRESS."

First Amendment to the U.S. Constitution

The basic foundation of our democracy is the First Amendment guarantee of freedom of expression. The Opposing Viewpoints Series is dedicated to the concept of this basic freedom and the idea that it is more important to practice it than to enshrine it.

CONTENTS

WHY CONSIDER OPPOSING VIEWPOINTS?

"The only way in which a human being can make some approach to knowing the whole of a subject is by hearing what can be said about it by persons of every variety of opinion and studying all modes in which it can be looked at by every character of mind. No wise man ever acquired his wisdom in any mode but this."

John Stuart Mill

In our media-intensive culture it is not difficult to find differing opinions. Thousands of newspapers and magazines and dozens of radio and television talk shows resound with differing points of view. The difficulty lies in deciding which opinion to agree with and which "experts" seem the most credible. The more inundated we become with differing opinions and claims, the more essential it is to hone critical reading and thinking skills to evaluate these ideas. Opposing Viewpoints books address this problem directly by presenting stimulating debates that can be used to enhance and teach these skills. The varied opinions contained in each book examine many different aspects of a single issue. While examining these conveniently edited opposing views, readers can develop critical thinking skills such as the ability to compare and contrast authors' credibility, facts, argumentation styles, use of persuasive techniques, and other stylistic tools. In short, the Opposing Viewpoints Series is an ideal way to attain the higher-level thinking and reading skills so essential in a culture of diverse and contradictory opinions.

In addition to providing a tool for critical thinking, Opposing Viewpoints books challenge readers to question their own strongly held opinions and assumptions. Most people form their opinions on the basis of upbringing, peer pressure, and personal, cultural, or professional bias. By reading carefully balanced opposing views, readers must directly confront new ideas as well as the opinions of those with whom they disagree. This is not to simplistically argue that everyone who reads opposing views will—or should—change his or her opinion. Instead, the series enhances readers' understanding of their own views by encouraging confrontation with opposing ideas. Careful examination of others' views can lead to the readers' understanding of the logical inconsistencies in their own opinions, perspective on why they hold an opinion, and the consideration of the possibility that their opinion requires further evaluation.

EVALUATING OTHER OPINIONS

To ensure that this type of examination occurs, Opposing Viewpoints books present all types of opinions. Prominent spokespeople on different sides of each issue as well as well-known professionals from many disciplines challenge the reader. An additional goal of the series is to provide a forum for other, less known, or even unpopular viewpoints. The opinion of an ordinary person who has had to make the decision to cut off life support from a terminally ill relative, for example, may be just as valuable and provide just as much insight as a medical ethicist's professional opinion. The editors have two additional purposes in including these less known views. One, the editors encourage readers to respect others' opinions—even when not enhanced by professional credibility. It is only by reading or listening to and objectively evaluating others' ideas that one can determine whether they are worthy of consideration. Two, the inclusion of such viewpoints encourages the important critical thinking skill of objectively evaluating an author's credentials and bias. This evaluation will illuminate an author's reasons for taking a particular stance on an issue and will aid in readers' evaluation of the author's ideas.

As series editors of the Opposing Viewpoints Series, it is our hope that these books will give readers a deeper understanding of the issues debated and an appreciation of the complexity of even seemingly simple issues when good and honest people disagree. This awareness is particularly important in a democratic society such as ours in which people enter into public debate to determine the common good. Those with whom one disagrees should not be regarded as enemies but rather as people whose views deserve careful examination and may shed light on one's own.

Thomas Jefferson once said that "difference of opinion leads to inquiry, and inquiry to truth." Jefferson, a broadly educated man, argued that "if a nation expects to be ignorant and free . . . it expects what never was and never will be." As individuals and as a nation, it is imperative that we consider the opinions of others and examine them with skill and discernment. The Opposing Viewpoints Series is intended to help readers achieve this goal.

David L. Bender & Bruno Leone,
Series Editors

Greenhaven Press anthologies primarily consist of previously published material taken from a variety of sources, including periodicals, books, scholarly journals, newspapers, government documents, and position papers from private and public organizations. These original sources are often edited for length and to ensure their accessibility for a young adult audience. The anthology editors also change the original titles of these works in order to clearly present the main thesis of each viewpoint and to explicitly indicate the opinion presented in the viewpoint. These alterations are made in consideration of both the reading and comprehension levels of a young adult audience. Every effort is made to ensure that Greenhaven Press accurately reflects the original intent of the authors included in this anthology.

INTRODUCTION

"There is a definite relationship between biological reality and gender identity."
—Robert Nadeau, professor of English at George Mason University

"Most of what we think of as essential differences between the sexes are actually the result of imposing different conditions on men and women."
—Joan Smith, journalist and author

The first thing most parents learn about their newborn is whether the child is a boy or a girl. From that moment, most of those children act in certain ways. Girls play with dolls and braid each other's hair, while boys play with trucks and get into fights. As the children grow up, the girls are expected to be more emotional and empathetic, while aggression is seen as a typical male trait. To some people, this behavior seems perfectly natural. However, debate exists over whether seemingly gender-specific behavior is a part of nature or is the result of social conditioning.

To some scientists and theorists, the biological differences between men and women make their gender roles inevitable. These "essentialists" contend that gender behavior is coded in the brain and in the chemistry of the body. Brain structure is cited as a key reason for gender differences. For example, neuroscientists have discovered that women's brains have a larger corpus callosum, which serves as the bridge that carries messages between the right and left hemispheres. Some theorists believe this difference in structure explains why women are more intuitive and better at expressing their emotions—the two hemispheres communicate more in women's brains, so information flows more readily from the emotional right hemisphere to the verbal left hemisphere. In addition to differences in the brain, other biological factors may play a part in shaping gender behavior. According to Clinton J. Jesser, a professor at Northern Illinois University: "There . . . appear to be genetic-hormonally based differences between the sexes in general perceptual/cognitive functions as well as . . . roughness in interpersonal contact and play (all higher for males) and, later, relational affinity to others." Hormones are believed to affect the genders in different ways, such as the way men and women respond to drugs or the association of testosterone with male aggression.

Essentialists also believe that, because of their sex, men and women have dissimilar attitudes toward marriage and procreation. Because pregnancy and motherhood are time-consuming and difficult, some analysts argue, it is natural for a woman to seek one partner who she thinks will be the best father and provider. On the other hand, impregnating a woman takes little time and effort for a man, so it is seen as biologically inevitable that a man will be more promiscuous. These biological differences further influence parenting as well. Mothers are believed to develop a relationship while the infant is still in the womb and during breastfeeding, making mothers more sensitive than fathers to the needs of nonverbal infants.

Other observers disagree that gender traits are encoded in the brain or in hormones. These experts believe that society shapes gender, pointing out that children are born into a society that has preexisting gender preferences and expectations. This view, known as social constructionism, asserts that children simply fulfill the biological image with which they identify. According to social constructionists, men and women behave differently because of social conditioning that is propagated by behaviors that are prevalent in society and reinforced by the media, family, and peers. For example, some analysts view articles in women's and girls' magazines as informing females how they should look and how they should behave. Advertisements are also seen as shaping and fostering gender stereotypes. Barbara Stern, a professor at Rutgers University in New Jersey, observes: "Stereotypes about sex-linked appropriate behaviors—including language—persist and are embodied in advertisements." She cites an advertisement for Merrill Lynch that portrayed a female financial consultant as nurturing and cooperative, while her male counterpart is described as aggressive and competitive.

Like their female counterparts, men and boys are bombarded with cultural messages, some writers contend. A boy who plays with Barbie dolls, or shows interest in other pursuits normally associated with girls, might be looked at askance, and his behavior may be corrected by peer pressure or even by parental persuasion. Columnist Katha Pollitt writes: "Could it be that even sports-resistant moms see athletics as part of manliness? That if their sons wanted to spend the weekend writing up their diaries, or reading, or baking, they'd find it disturbing?" Studies show that teachers and peers also teach boys at any early age what type of behavior to avoid or embrace; boys are kept away from the dolls and the play kitchens, note Nigel Edley and Margaret Wetherell, the co-authors of *Men in Perspective: Practice, Power and Iden-*

tity. These cultural messages can have their downside, some social constructionists note. Phyllis Burke, the author of *Gender Shock: Exploding the Myths of Male and Female*, writes: "Male researchers have now found that the masculine sex role is significantly related to psychological stress, and that the condition driving gender role conflict in men is a deep fear of being, or appearing, feminine."

However, the essentialist and social constructionist views are not incompatible. Most theorists contend that biology and sociology are, if not equally influential in determining gender behavior, then at least inseparable. Deborah Blum, a professor at the University of Wisconsin at Madison, observes that the testosterone levels of female lawyers or police officers are higher than those of stay-at-home mothers. She notes that one cannot ascertain whether the testosterone level influenced the career choice or vice versa, thus indicating how biological and social forces cannot be wholly separated. In fact, the exact influence may never be known because gender expectations are forced on individuals at an early age. Edley and Wetherell cite studies that show parents treat boys and girls differently from the day of birth, even decorating the bedrooms of newborns with gender-specific wallpaper. As a result, the authors note, "It becomes virtually impossible to decide whether a particular behavioural sex difference is the result of biological factors or differential parental treatment."

Some physical differences between men and women are undeniable. But universal explanations do not exist for all gender differences, great or small. *Male/Female Roles: Opposing Viewpoints* considers the behavior of men and women in the following chapters: How Are Gender Roles Established? Have Women's Roles Changed for the Better? Have Men's Roles Changed for the Better? What Will Improve Male/Female Relationships? In these chapters, the authors debate whether men and women have naturally distinct roles or if these roles are part of social expectations.

CHAPTER 1

HOW ARE GENDER ROLES ESTABLISHED?

CHAPTER PREFACE

In the 1960s, the penis of an eight-month-old boy was accidentally destroyed during minor surgery. His parents were told by a doctor to raise the boy as a girl and surgery was performed to create female anatomy. At first, this surgery was considered a success and reported in medical journals as proof that sex-reassignment surgery was viable. However, three decades later it was revealed that the child—known pseudonymously as John/Joan—had always thought of himself as a boy, despite being dressed in girl's clothes and raised as a girl. John/Joan wanted to learn how to shave, played with his twin brother's toys, and voiced interest in being a garbage collector. When he was a teenager, his father told John/Joan about the surgery, and the boy underwent a sex change to return to his birth gender. Although unable to father children, John eventually married and adopted his wife's children. Critics of sex-reassignment surgery cite this case as proof that gender identity is part of an individual's biology or "nature" and not something that is learned through observance of social conventions. Doctors Kenneth Kipnis and Milton Diamond, writing about the case, observe: "Though Joan learned all she was supposed to, her behavior nonetheless exhibited quintessential male elements. . . . Feminine social imprinting did not occur."

But even with such a compelling case, some scholars believe that it is not biology that determines sexual identity. They contend that social and cultural messages also influence—or "nurture"—gender. According to Deborah L. Rhode, a law professor who has written on gender issues, parents, teachers, and the media are key influences in creating gender identity. For example, she argues, parents prefer that their children play with gender-appropriate toys. "Although over four-fifths of surveyed parents say that it is important for children to play with toys of all kinds, they provide more approval for 'sex-appropriate' choices," she writes. Because parents and the rest of society have culturally constructed views of typical and appropriate gender behavior, they consciously or unconsciously convey these expectations to children. The children are usually eager to fulfill the expectations, Rhode contends.

A consensus may never be reached in the debate over whether nature or nurture has the greatest influence in determining gender. In the following chapter, the authors propose various biological and cultural aspects of identity that may shape gender roles.

"Male and female differences,
physical, emotional and mental, are
biological, not environmental."

BIOLOGICAL DIFFERENCES ESTABLISH GENDER ROLES

Charley Reese

In the following viewpoint, Charley Reese argues that, contrary to the belief of feminists, gender is determined by biology and not by environment. In cautioning against those who would ignore the biological differences that shape their gender, he cites the case of Shannon Faulkner. The first woman allowed to enroll in the Citadel—a South Carolina military college—Faulkner dropped out soon after her entrance, citing stress and exhaustion. According to Reese, Faulkner made the correct decision in leaving the Citadel because she heeded her inherent nature. Reese is a syndicated columnist.

As you read, consider the following questions:

1. According to Reese, what are some mental skills in which men are superior to women?
2. In the author's view, what type of women can physically keep up with men?
3. What does Reese think has caused many of the twentieth century's problems?

Reprinted from Charley Reese, "Faulkner Was Feminists' Pawn," *Conservative Chronicle*, September 13, 1995, with special permission from King Features Syndicate.

I don't know which has been sadder—watching young Shannon Faulkner decide that, after all, she really didn't want to be a Citadel cadet or the fire-hosing of venom on both Faulkner and the Citadel by feminists and male feminist-panderers.

Actually, both Shannon Faulkner and the Citadel are simply victims of feminist ideology that is based on a false premise—namely, that differences between men and women are a result of social conditioning.

DIFFERENCES ARE BIOLOGICAL

There is a ton of medical studies which disprove that idiotic notion. Male and female differences, physical, emotional and mental, are biological, not environmental.

Men have greater size and strength, a greater capacity for short-term energy output; women have lesser size and strength but a greater capacity for endurance. Mentally, men are better at spatial and mathematical skills and logic; women are better at verbal and social skills and empathy.

Temperamentally, men are inclined toward dominance, rank-related aggression (competitiveness), independence, psychopathy and sensation-seeking. Women are inclined toward submission, defensive aggression, attachment and nurturance, anxiety and security-seeking.

These characteristics are taken from studies by Symons, 1979; Seward and Seward, 1980; and Ellis, 1986. All are quoted in the 1989 book The *Great Sex Divide*, by Dr. Glenn Wilson, senior lecturer in psychology at the Institute of Psychiatry, University of London. Scott-Townsend is the publisher.

CONTROLLED BY GENES

The point is that Faulkner was used as pawn by feminists to make an ideological Brownie point, but in the end, she listened to her inherent nature and quit an environment to which she is not suited. No one should blame her or find fault with her. In leaving, she did the right thing.

As much as an affront to our dignity as it may be, we are all at the mercy of genes and hormones to a much larger extent than social determinists are willing to admit, though by now, social determinism is pretty much a flat-earth theory held only by intellectual reactionaries.

To head off those who always cite the exceptions, I will remind you that the characteristic of nature is profusion, not uniformity. There are certainly some women who can keep up with the boys—but they will have narrow pelvises and greater amounts of male hormones than the average.

Conversely, there are men with wider pelvises and more female hormones who tend to exhibit certain female characteristics, such as passiveness.

WOMEN'S NATURE IS DIFFERENT FROM MEN'S

Feminism has been at war with human nature from the beginning, and nowhere more so than in its fierce campaign against motherhood. Babies and children, feminists rightly perceive, are what make women's lives dramatically, unalterably different from men's. For the past three decades, feminist scholars and writers have attempted to prove that our roles as parents, like our roles in the workplace, are interchangeable with men's.

Biology, however, has persistently behaved like an impolite relative who will not leave a family event. For example, a Harvard Medical School study reported in 1997 that women undergoing infertility treatments had levels of depression comparable to patients with AIDS and cancer. Alas, it isn't social conditioning that makes women grieve this way. It is written into our DNA.

Mona Charen, *Women's Quarterly*, Spring 1998.

Actually, radical feminists are doing the same thing homophobes do: They beat up on and bully women for something they can't help—being women. Nature doesn't give a flea's hind leg for our social theories, fads, fashions, political ideologies and other nutty ideas with which people preoccupy themselves. Nature just is. And all of us are part of it whether we like it or not.

DO NOT FIGHT NATURE

A source of much of the 20th century's madness, cruelty and bloodshed has been the result of the refusal to live in accordance with nature or to even recognize its reality. Any time we are out of sync with nature, we, not nature, will be the loser and the sufferer.

We must adapt to reality; reality will not adapt to us or allow us to shape it. That's what Shannon Faulkner discovered when she met the reality, as opposed to the theory, of being a cadet at the Citadel.

CRACKPOT FEMINISM

Feminism in the United States is a current mania. The combination of mediocre minds and cowardice is a fertile field in which to grow all kinds of manias, cockamamie theories and ideologies.

Nevertheless, feminism needs to be dragged and dropped into the ashcan of crackpot ideas. It has nothing whatsoever to do with real people and nothing to offer people except miserable carping and undeserved guilt trips.

Neither Shannon Faulkner nor the Citadel deserves any criticism.

| "Children receive strong cultural messages about sex-appropriate traits, tasks, and behaviors."

CULTURE ESTABLISHES GENDER ROLES

Deborah L. Rhode

Gender roles in children are shaped by cultural forces, argues Deborah L. Rhode in the following viewpoint. She asserts that children are taught gender stereotypes by their peers and adults—for example, girls learn to be nurturing and boys are expected to be aggressive. According to Rhode, these messages, intentional or otherwise, are widespread. Rhode is the Ernest W. McFarland Professor of Law at Stanford University in Palo Alto, California, and the author of *Speaking of Sex: The Denial of Gender Inequality*, from which this viewpoint is taken.

As you read, consider the following questions:

1. According to a survey of Michigan elementary students, as cited by Rhode, what percentage of girls thought there were advantages to being male?
2. By what age do children have sex-linked toy preferences, according to the author?
3. As stated by Rhode, what is Nancy Chodorow and Dorothy Dinnerstein's theory on how gender identity is formed?

M ost research makes clear that whatever their biological predispositions, children receive strong cultural messages about sex-appropriate traits, tasks, and behaviors. These messages often involve unconscious, subtle, or indirect signals, rather than intentional instruction. Until adults become more aware of their role in the gender socialization process, we cannot reverse its most damaging effects.

AMBIVALENCE OVER EQUALITY

A threshold challenge lies in convincing the public that there is any significant problem to address. On this point, Americans are ambivalent. At least in principle, the vast majority of parents and educators support equality between the sexes and want children to develop their full potential. Yet most adults are uncomfortable with the prospect of a world without significant gender differences and are not preparing their children to live in one.

Nor are many adults aware of the systematic gender inequalities that begin at early ages. Several studies documenting such inequalities have triggered waves of denial. Conservative commentators have had a field day with "the facts." Why should self-appointed "sex equity bureaucrats" be whining when girls get better grades, earn more high school degrees, and have lower rates of adolescent suicide, delinquency, and drug abuse? Yet such patterns are hardly an endorsement of current childrearing. Rather, they make clear that prevailing practices carry costs for both sexes. Moreover, too many Americans discount the disproportionate price that girls eventually pay for gender stereotypes. . . . On almost all dimensions of power, status, income, and physical security, women end up worse off than men. And . . . those inequalities build on roles learned in childhood.

Indeed, children themselves are aware of gender hierarchies, well before any bureaucrats bombard them with the relevant statistics. When 1,100 Michigan elementary students were asked to describe what life would be like if they were the opposite sex, over 40 percent of the girls saw advantages to being male; they would have better jobs, higher incomes, and more respect. Ninety-five percent of the boys saw no advantage to being female, and a substantial number thought suicide would be preferable. If we want to alter such gender hierarchies, we need a better understanding of how and where they start.

GENDER IDENTITY AND GENDER ROLES

Sandra Bem, a leading expert on sex stereotypes, describes the efforts she made to free her son from traditional assumptions. At every opportunity, she emphasized that the only "real" differences between the sexes were anatomical and also encouraged his interests in "feminine" toys and activities. The difficulty of her task became clear the day that he decided to wear a barrette to nursery school. His appearance provoked an immediate argument with a classmate who insisted that "boys don't wear barrettes." Bem's son responded with a lecture on real differences, which he illustrated by dropping his trousers and displaying the evidence. His fellow four-year-old was unpersuaded. "Everybody has a penis," he insisted, "only girls wear barrettes."

Such dialogues highlight the cultural underpinnings of sex-based roles. Children develop a strong sense of gender identity many years before they associate it with anatomical differences. By age two, toddlers have sex-linked toy preferences; by age three they can identify certain occupations as more appropriate for each sex; and between ages four and six they separate into same-sex groups with distinctive play patterns and rigid assumptions about appropriate male and female behavior.

CHOOSING WHICH MESSAGE TO SEND

Feminists are often accused of imposing their "agenda" on children. Isn't that what adults always do, consciously and unconsciously? Kids aren't born religious, or polite, or kind, or able to remember where they put their sneakers. Inculcating these behaviors, and the values behind them, is a tremendous amount of work, involving many adults. We don't have a choice, really, about whether we should give our children messages about what it means to be male and female—they're bombarded with them from morning till night.

The question, as always, is what do we want those messages to be?

Katha Pollitt, New York Times Magazine, October 8, 1995.

Throughout childhood, gender segregation serves to reinforce gender stereotypes. Boys' activities celebrate heroism and involve rough-and-tumble activities; they reward dominance, competitiveness, and aggression. Girls' activities make romance and domesticity a far more common theme, and their play is more attentive to relationships and personal appearance. In these contexts, the most vigilant policing of sex stereotypes comes from other children. Boys are particularly intolerant of any perceived deviance, and the scorn they direct at "fags" and "sissies" reinforces conventional norms of masculinity and persistent patterns of homophobia.

THE FORMATION OF STEREOTYPES

The causes of such rigid gender stereotyping remain unclear. Some researchers believe that physiological differences in hormonal levels, in spatial and perceptual capacities, and in verbal development patterns help explain sex-linked styles of play. Other contemporary experts offer psychoanalytic explanations, although typically not the classical Freudian accounts of penis envy and castration complexes. For example, feminist theorists such as Nancy Chodorow and Dorothy Dinnerstein stress children's relation to their primary caretaker as the foundation for gender identity. Because these caretakers generally are women, girls learn to see themselves as similar and fundamentally connected to others, while boys learn to see themselves as separate and different. Under this view, such developmental processes encourage nurturing and interpersonal skills in girls and assertiveness and independence in boys.

Still other theorists stress cognitive and social learning. Their emphasis is on the strategies of imitation, observation, and reinforcement that underpin gender identity. For individuals concerned with gender inequality, these generally are the processes of greatest interest. Compared with psychoanalytic and sociobiological frameworks, social-learning theories are more responsive to context and therefore more able to account for variations over time, culture, class, race, and ethnicity. A focus on social learning also highlights the cultural forces that are most open to change.

Even theorists wedded to biological and psychoanalytic explanations acknowledge that social learning plays a crucial role in shaping sex-linked behaviors. Whatever children's predispositions, they also receive frequent signals from parents, peers, teachers, and the media. In countless ways, our culture encourages boys to be assertive, competitive, and independent—to make things work and happen. We tell girls to be nice, caring, and dependent—to worry about how they look and what others feel. Females learn how to get along; males learn how to get ahead. And children of both sexes learn, above all, that gender matters. Toys, clothing, occupations, household tasks, even pronouns differ according to sex. The cues are everywhere, and children pick up many messages that we neither notice nor intend.

| "If there is indeed a biology to sex differences, we amplify it."

BOTH BIOLOGY AND CULTURE HELP ESTABLISH GENDER ROLES

Deborah Blum

In the following viewpoint, Deborah Blum contends that while biological differences play a part in forming gender roles, those differences are amplified by cultural and environmental influences. She maintains that certain biological disparities, such as testosterone's part in making men more aggressive, do influence personality. However, Blum argues, these biological differences are tempered by factors such as a person's upbringing and work environment. Blum is a professor of journalism at the University of Wisconsin in Madison and the author of *Sex on the Brain: The Biological Differences Between Men and Women.*

As you read, consider the following questions:

1. According to statistics cited by Blum, in conflicts in which a woman killed a man, how often did the man start the fight?
2. In the author's view, at what age will a child who is raised in a less traditional family develop a traditional sense of gender roles?
3. What happens to the testosterone level of a person who loses a game, according to Blum?

Excerpted from Deborah Blum, "The Gender Blur," *Utne Reader*, September/October 1998. Reprinted with permission from the author.

One of the reasons we're so fascinated by childhood behaviors is that, as the old saying goes, the child becomes the man (or woman, of course.) Most girls don't spend their preschool years snarling around the house and pretending to chew off their companion's legs. And they—mostly—don't grow up to be as aggressive as men. Do the ways that we amplify those early differences in childhood shape the adults we become? Absolutely. But it's worth exploring the starting place—the faint signal that somehow gets amplified.

"There's plenty of room in society to influence sex differences," says Marc Breedlove, a behavioral endocrinologist at the University of California at Berkeley and a pioneer in defining how hormones can help build sexually different nervous systems. "Yes, we're born with predispositions, but it's society that amplifies them, exaggerates them. I believe that—except for the sex differences in aggression. Those [differences] are too massive to be explained simply by society."

MEN ARE MORE AGGRESSIVE

Aggression does allow a straightforward look at the issue. Consider the following statistics: Crime reports in both the United States and Europe record between 10 and 15 robberies committed by men for every one by a woman. At one point, people argued that this was explained by size difference. Women weren't big enough to intimidate, but that would change, they predicted, with the availability of compact weapons. But just as little girls don't routinely make weapons out of toast, women—even criminal ones—don't seem drawn to weaponry in the same way that men are. Almost twice as many male thieves and robbers use guns as their female counterparts do.

Or you can look at more personal crimes: domestic partner murders. Three-fourths of men use guns in those killings; 50 percent of women do. Here's more from the domestic front: In conflicts in which a woman killed a man, he tended to be the one who had started the fight—in 51.8 percent of the cases, to be exact. When the man was the killer, he again was the likely first aggressor, and by an even more dramatic margin. In fights in which women died, they had started the argument only 12.5 percent of the time.

Enough. You can parade endless similar statistics but the point is this: Males are more aggressive, not just among humans but among almost all species on earth. . . .

Thus the issue becomes not whether there is a biologically influenced sex difference in aggression—the answer being a solid, technical "You betcha"—but rather how rigid that difference is. The best science, in my opinion, tends to align with basic common sense. We all know that there are extraordinarily gentle men and murderous women. Sex differences are always generalizations: They refer to a behavior, with some evolutionary rationale behind it. They never define, entirely, an individual. And that fact alone should tell us that there's always—even in the most biologically dominated traits—some flexibility, an instinctive ability to respond, for better and worse, to the world around us.

This is true even with physical characteristics that we've often assumed are nailed down by genetics. Scientists now believe height, for instance, is only about 90 percent heritable. A person's genes might code for a six-foot-tall body, but malnutrition could literally cut that short. And there's also some evidence, in girls anyway, that children with stressful childhoods tend to become shorter adults. So while some factors are predetermined, there's evidence that the prototypical male/female body design can be readily altered.

It's a given that humans, like most other species—bananas, spiders, sharks, ducks, any rabbit you pull out of a hat—rely on two sexes for reproduction. So basic is that requirement that we have chromosomes whose primary purpose is to deliver the genes that order up a male or a female. All other chromosomes are numbered, but we label the sex chromosomes with the letters X and Y. We get one each from our mother and our father, and the basic combinations are these: XX makes female, XY makes male.

There are two important—and little known—points about these chromosomal matches. One is that even with this apparently precise system, there's nothing precise—or guaranteed— about the physical construction of male and female. The other point makes that possible. It appears that sex doesn't matter in the early stages of embryonic development. We are unisex at the point of conception. . . .

THE IMPACT OF TESTOSTERONE

Do the ways that we amplify physical and behavioral differences in childhood shape who we become as adults? Absolutely. But to understand that, you have to understand the differences themselves—their beginning and the very real biochemistry that may lie behind them.

Here is a good place to focus on testosterone—a hormone that is both well-studied and generally underrated. First, however, I want to acknowledge that there are many other hormones and neurotransmitters that appear to influence behavior. Preliminary work shows that fetal boys are a little more active than fetal girls. It's pretty difficult to argue socialization at that point. There's a strong suspicion that testosterone may create the difference. And there are a couple of relevant animal models to emphasize the point. Back in the 1960s, Robert Goy, a psychologist at the University of Wisconsin at Madison, first documented that young male monkeys play much more roughly than young females. Goy went on to show that if you manipulate testosterone level—raising it in females, damping it down in males—you can reverse those effects, creating sweet little male monkeys and rowdy young females.

Social Constructionists and Essentialists

Social constructionist explanations of contemporary sexual patterns are typically pitted against the biology of desire and the evolutionary understanding of biological adaptations. Some social constructionists believe there is no inflexible biological reality; everything we regard as either female or male sexuality is culturally imposed. In contrast, essentialists—those who take a biological, sociobiological, or evolutionary point of view—believe people's sexual desires and orientations are innate and hard-wired and that social impact is minimal. Gender differences follow from reproductive differences. . . .

Using either the social constructionist or essentialist approach to the exclusion of the other constrains understanding of sexuality. We believe the evidence shows that gender differences are more plausibly an outcome of social processes than the other way around. But a social constructionist view is most powerful when it takes the essentialist view into account.

Pepper Schwartz and Virginia Rutter, *The Gender of Sexuality*, Thousand Oaks, CA: Pine Forge Press, 1998.

Is testosterone the only factor at work here? I don't think so. But clearly we can argue a strong influence, and, interestingly, studies have found that girls with congenital adrenal hypoplasia—who run high in testosterone—tend to be far more fascinated by trucks and toy weaponry than most little girls are. They lean toward rough-and-tumble play, too. As it turns out, the strongest influence on this "abnormal" behavior is not parental disapproval, but the company of other little girls, who tone them down and direct them toward more routine girl games.

And that reinforces an early point: If there is indeed a biology to sex differences, we amplify it. At some point—when it is still up for debate—we gain a sense of our gender, and with it a sense of "gender-appropriate" behavior.

Some scientists argue for some evidence of gender awareness in infancy, perhaps by the age of 12 months. The consensus seems to be that full-blown "I'm a girl" or "I'm a boy" instincts arrive between the ages of 2 and 3. Research shows that if a family operates in a very traditional, Beaver Cleaver kind of environment, filled with awareness of and association with "proper" gender behaviors the "boys do trucks, girls do dolls" attitude seems to come very early. If a child grows up in a less traditional family, with an emphasis on partnership and sharing—"We all do the dishes, Joshua"—children maintain a more flexible sense of gender roles until about age 6. . . .

BIOLOGY IS RESPONSIVE

How does all this fit together—toys and testosterone, biology and behavior, the development of the child into the adult, the way that men and women relate to one another?

Let me make a cautious statement about testosterone: It not only has some body-building functions, it influences some behaviors as well. Let's make that a little less cautious: These behaviors include rowdy play, sex drive, competitiveness, and an in-your-face attitude. Males tend to have a higher baseline of testosterone than females—in our species, about seven to ten times as much—and therefore you would predict (correctly, I think) that all of those behaviors would be more generally found in men than in women.

But testosterone is also one of my favorite examples of how responsive biology is, how attuned it is to the way we live our lives. Testosterone, it turns out, rises in response to competition and threat. In the days of our ancestors, this might have been hand-to-hand combat or high-risk hunting endeavors. Today, scientists have measured testosterone rise in athletes preparing for a game, in chess players awaiting a match, in spectators following a soccer competition.

If a person—or even just a person's favored team—wins, testosterone continues to rise. It falls with a loss. (This also makes sense in an evolutionary perspective. If one was being clobbered with a club, it would be extremely unhelpful to have a hormone urging one to battle on.) Testosterone also rises in the competitive world of dating, settles down with a stable and supportive relationship, climbs again if the relationship starts to falter.

It's been known for years that men in high-stress professions—say, police work or corporate law—have higher testosterone levels than men in the ministry. It turns out that women in the same kind of strong-attitude professions have higher testosterone than women who choose to stay home. What I like about this is the chicken-or-egg aspect. If you argue that testosterone influenced the behavior of those women, which came first? Did they have high testosterone and choose the law? Or did they choose the law, and the competitive environment ratcheted them up on the androgen scale? Or could both be at work?

And, returning to children for a moment, there's an ongoing study by Pennsylvania researchers, tracking that question in adolescent girls, who are being encouraged by their parents to engage in competitive activities that were once for boys only. As they do so, the researchers are monitoring, regularly, two hormones: testosterone and cortisol, a stress hormone. Will these hormones rise in response to this new, more traditionally male environment? What if more girls choose the competitive path; more boys choose the other? Will female testosterone levels rise, male levels fall? Will that wonderful, unpredictable, flexible biology that we've been given allow a shift, so that one day, we will literally be far more alike?

We may not have answers to all those questions but we can ask them, and we can expect that the answers will come someday, because science clearly shows us that such possibilities exist. In this most important sense, sex differences offer us a paradox. It is only through exploring and understanding what makes us different that we can begin to understand what binds us together.

"The brains of males and females are constructed differently."

BRAIN STRUCTURE EXPLAINS MALE/FEMALE DIFFERENCES

John Leo

In the following viewpoint, John Leo contends that men and women have dissimilar interests and abilities due to differences in their brain structure. He cites a study that indicates men and women use their left and right brain hemispheres differently. As a result, Leo argues, women are better at expressing emotions while men have superior spatial abilities. According to Leo, however, American culture has yet to fully accept these biological differences. Leo is a contributing editor at *U.S. News & World Report*.

As you read, consider the following questions:

1. How did the feminism of the 1970s believe sexual equality could be achieved, in Leo's view?
2. According to the author, why are men less able to express emotions?
3. According to Leo, what percentage of American girls in elementary school reach the average level of male performance in tests of spatial ability?

An old story made Page 1 news in the *New York Times* [in February 1995]: "Men and Women Use Brain Differently, Study Discovers." That headline could have run over a roughly similar story any time during the 1980s. An enormous heap of scientific evidence on sexual differences has been accumulating for 15 years or more. Yet this story probably deserved front-page treatment because of the significant photo that ran alongside it.

MEN AND WOMEN HAVE DIFFERENT BRAINS

Old news: The brains of males and females are constructed differently, resulting in important differences in perceptions, emotional expression, priorities and behavior. "The truth is that virtually every professional scientist and researcher into the subject has reached that conclusion," Anne Moir and David Jessel wrote in 1991 in their book, *Brain Sex*.

Despite this evidence, American culture still seems to operate on the broad assumption that sexual differences are unimportant, and that male and female brains essentially function the same way.

In part, this is because of the civil-rights approach to the rise of women in the work force. The vocabulary of this approach, borrowed from the race issue, tends to assume that any "underrepresentation" of women in any area must be due to oppression and bias, never to the free choice of women who may not be attracted to certain activities in the same numbers as men. Linking race (no proven brain differences) to sex (many proven differences) has guaranteed a large amount of confusion.

DENYING THE DIFFERENCES

In part, too, the denial of differences is a holdover from the feminism of the 1970s, which generally felt that sexual equality depended on minimizing or denying sexual differences. Even talking about sexual differences came to be seen as something of a betrayal of the women's movement. This older view was displayed on national television in early 1995 when Gloria Steinem told ABC's John Stossel that sexual differences shouldn't even be studied. (This is a classic head-in-the-sand idea, but let's admit that women have historic reasons to be wary of research into this area. It has been used repeatedly to restrict the kind of jobs open to women.)

So side by side, we have a large body of evidence, and a curious refusal, based on politics, to acknowledge it.

The photo that ran with the study may help break down this resistance. It's a magnetic resonance image of a male brain and a female brain attempting the same task—sounding out words. The image—apparently the first graphic, visual proof of difference in the brains—shows that the male used only a small part of the left side of the brain, while the female used both sides.

EMOTIONAL AND LINGUISTIC DIFFERENCES

The two halves of the male brain are connected by a smaller number of fibers than the female's, and some scientists think this may help explain the male's famous inability to express emotions: Information flows less easily from the right side to the verbal, left side.

The lead researcher on the project, Sally Shaywitz of Yale University's School of Medicine, said she was surprised to see sexual differences in decoding words, "the pinnacle of what humans do," far removed from the basic evolutionary pressures that produced different brain structures in males and females. The implication is that this is the tip of the iceberg—many more differences will show up in future scans.

© Steve Kelley. Reprinted with permission.

The culture seems on the brink of yet another of those large psychic shifts. Popular bestsellers have begun to emphasize differences, not sameness: *Men Are From Mars, Women Are From Venus*, for instance, or Deborah Tannen's books. In the intellectual world, the long dominant idea that biology doesn't matter much (because human culture is so powerful) is starting to come under heavy attack.

"Difference feminists" argue that women's "ethic of care" makes them radically different from men, and perhaps superior. The new glamorization of women's colleges is partly due to identity politics, partly to irritation with men, partly to the idea that women and men have wholly different methods of learning. Ursuline College now offers a curriculum based on "women's way of knowing."

FUTURE ARGUMENTS

Two kinds of arguments are on the horizon. Are sexual stereotypes about to be smuggled back in under cover of science? And if the sexes excel in different areas, is the public ready for the reality that some high-prestige, high-paying fields will be 75 percent male, some 75 percent female?

The studies clearly show a large male advantage in visual-spatial abilities and higher mathematical reasoning. Every social explanation has been exhausted—this is innate. Only about 20 percent of American girls in elementary grades reach the average level of male performance in tests of spatial ability. And the U.S. Employment Service says that all classes of engineering and most scientific and technical occupations require spatial ability found in the top 10 percent of the population.

The best course of action would be to open all the doors and let girls and boys compete wherever they wish, without demanding anything like sexual quotas. But in a culture where males still hold most of the best jobs, this best course will be hard to defend.

| "There is much more overlap than
  difference in the sexes' abilities."

THE ROLE OF BRAIN STRUCTURE
IS OVERSTATED

Miranda Spencer

In the following viewpoint, Miranda Spencer argues that the influence of brain structure in explaining gender differences is less extensive than some journalists suggest. She criticizes a television program that claimed to prove men and women have different abilities due to their biology, arguing that the evidence presented by ABC correspondent John Stossel was unbalanced and misleading. According to Spencer, the program ignored studies that indicated there is greater overlap than difference in the aptitudes of men and women. Spencer is a freelance reporter and editor.

As you read, consider the following questions:

1. In Spencer's opinion, how were the views of Gloria Steinem and Bella Abzug framed in the ABC program?
2. According to the author, how did Stossel "reinterpret" videotape of children playing with Mighty Morphin Power Ranger dolls?
3. How has science been used to explain women's place, according to Spencer?

Reprinted from Miranda Spencer, "Desperately Seeking Difference: ABC Finds Biology Is Destiny," *Extra!* May/June 1995, by permission of the author.

With the [February 1995] ABC News special, *Boys and Girls Are Different: Men, Women and the Sex Difference*, reported by correspondent John Stossel, hormonally induced haircut prices joined gay brains and race-based IQ as the politically charged science of the media moment.

The show asked the eternal question, "Are men and women supposed to be the same, or are we different creatures right from birth?" Stossel argued that any remnants of sexism in today's egalitarian society can't explain noticeable sex differences in our behavior ("men are obsessed with sports, women have more friends"), nor account for women's failure to reach economic parity and political power. But, he averred, science can.

SCIENTIFIC CLAIMS

"Quieter voices . . . are saying what parents and others, sexist or not, have been saying for years," Stossel declared. Animal studies show mother monkeys do all the nurturing, and "they aren't watching sexist TV." Anthropology answers why girls have finger dexterity and boys can visualize in 3-D. Prehistoric women gathered seeds and berries while men hunted the plains with spears; evolution hard-wired these skills in our skulls.

"If we think differently because our brains are different," Stossel concluded, "then trying to fix these differences will be pointless, expensive, even hurtful." Stossel attacked sex discrimination lawsuits, affirmative action and other remedies for inequality as "forcing" business and institutions to numerically balance the scales.

To back up his sweeping claims, Stossel quoted psychologists, geneticists, anthropologists and other scientists to support hormonal, neurological and evolutionary explanations for differing gender traits and roles. To give a superficial impression of balance, he brought in non-scientists—women identified with the feminist movement, like Gloria Steinem and Bella Abzug—to argue against them. Their opinions, however, were framed as calls for censorship and utopian social engineering. As the tabloid-style announcer introducing the program put it: "Should gender influence our place in society? Some research says yes. Some people don't want you to hear about it."

Ordinary people—like a perplexed parent who told of sons who "made guns out of carrots and cucumbers"—were brought on to back up the scientists who argued for essential differences.

DELIBERATE IGNORANCE

Totally missing were the many scientists whose research and writing have criticized biological explanations of sex differences.

These include two of the most prominent names in the field of gender studies: Brown University biologist Anne Fausto-Sterling, author of *Myths of Gender: Biological Theories About Men and Women*, and social psychologist Carol Tavris, author of *The Mismeasure of Woman: Why Women Are Not the Better Sex, the Inferior Sex, or the Opposite Sex*.

Fausto-Sterling, Tavris and others have pointed out that there is much more overlap than difference in the sexes' abilities; diversity, not dichotomy, between men and women's perceptions and behavior is the rule. They point out that the differences which many modern studies set out to understand are quite small, and often subtle, in the first place.

ABC was aware that these different scientific viewpoints existed; fact-checkers for the program contacted Fausto-Sterling and other like-minded researchers before the show aired. One ABC producer told Fausto-Sterling that interviews were already "set up" and that it was too late to restructure the show to introduce more balance. Joan Bertin, co-director of Columbia University's Program on Gender, Science and Law, was also called by an ABC staffer who had no interest in material that didn't fit in with Stossel's preconceived thesis. "She left me with the clear impression she had explicit marching orders to find material to support gender differences," Bertin told [bimonthly magazine of media criticism] EXTRA!.

MISLEADING STUDIES

Studies [on male and female brains] give the impression that all men have one brain structure and all women another, but that is not true. There is a gradation of brain structures in men as there is in women, even in the corpus callosum, and the differences are more significant among men, and among women, than between men and women.

Men's and women's bodies are different because of reproductive design. Differences based on reproductivity, however, do not generalize to the ability to shoot a gun or wash a baby. Primary and secondary sex characteristics, such as body hair, wombs and testes, do not establish spatial or verbal abilities. Yet researchers continue to troll for sex differences and bankable headlines.

Phyllis Burke, *Gender Shock: Exploding the Myths of Male and Female*, 1996.

This deliberate ignorance of opposing scientific views allowed Stossel to pose as the defender of objective truth, contrasting himself with those who tailor the truth to fit their preconceived ideological notions: "If we deny what science knows about human nature, how can we create sensible social policies? Isn't it better to act on the basis of what is true, rather than maintaining it has no right to be true?"

By not including a range of scientists in his reporting, Stossel ignored a wealth of research that provides non-biological explanations for differences between men and women. Entire disciplines, including educational psychology and cognitive science, were snubbed.

Beverly Fagot, a professor of psychology at the University of Oregon, for example, has done studies showing how boys' and girls' behavior differences reflect their ability to understand "gender schema"—kids' mental concept of which sex they are and how that sex is "supposed to" act. Schema for gender emerges at a very young age, but it's only a phase of development. Hence, sex differences seem most pronounced among children, but diminish over time.

VIDEO DISTORTIONS

Rather than acknowledging the existence of contrary data, Stossel hyped studies that seemed to back up his thesis (ignoring challenges by other researchers to these studies' methodology, assumptions and significance). Though the atmosphere of a television studio hardly replicates that of a controlled laboratory, ABC repeatedly dramatized (i.e., restaged) the studies in question, perhaps to give viewers the illusion they were eyewitnesses to the very experiments proving differences.

Indeed, at the end of the program, Stossel admitted he had aired footage that distorted what he himself had witnessed in one of the video "studies." In the beginning and middle of the show, viewers saw footage of toddlers separated from parents by a clear barrier, while Stossel narrated: "Most boys try to knock the barrier down. Most girls just stand there and cry for help." At the end of the show, Stossel ran footage showing the same experiment—only it was the girls who were aggressive and the tearful, passive babies were boys. "On the day we taped, it happened that we saw only the exceptions," he admitted.

If the video didn't show what Stossel wanted it to, it could be reinterpreted. "Boys play with action figures," Stossel claimed, illustrating this with a shot of a boy playing with a Mighty Morphin Power Ranger. Later, to make the point that "girls play with dolls," a girl was shown . . . playing with a Power Ranger.

To validate the stereotype that "women have trouble with maps, but remember landmarks. . . . Men won't ask for directions," Stossel offered a dramatization—not identified as such—of a bickering couple on a car trip. ("I don't think this map shows where we are at all," the woman wails.) Bolstered by the "evidence" provided by these actors, Stossel leaps to the idea that "maybe it's right" that few women are engineers and chess champs.

Likewise, dry-cleaners may be entitled to charge higher prices to clean women's blouses, because female customers are "more demanding. . . . This is consistent with the scientific research that shows women have better proximal sense, like . . . better close-up vision."

BEAUTIFUL MARKETS

Perhaps the report's biggest omission of all was Stossel's own bias. A self-professed free market libertarian, it's Stossel's loudly stated stand that "markets are magical and the best protectors of the consumer. It is my job to explain the beauties of the free market," he told the *Oregonian* (10/26/94). And the "beauties of the free market" are heavily promoted in Stossel's reporting—to the exclusion of contradictory evidence. Two out of three producers working on a previous Stossel special, *Are We Scaring Ourselves to Death?*, resigned because their research did not support Stossel's pro-industry prejudices (*EXTRA! Update*, 6/94).

As in Stossel's other recent reports, *Boys and Girls* presents protection of corporations as consumer protection. "Legal fees will . . . be passed on to you if you or your kids take an SAT test. Boys do better on these tests, especially in math, so lawyers from the ACLU say there have to be changes." In fact, a federal judge ruled that the aptitude exam was gender-biased because its results do not accurately predict women's performance in college—which is what the aptitude test is supposed to do.

Stossel presented equal-rights lawyers as virtual ambulance-chasers, out to make a buck on frivolous suits: "Oh, yes, and more lawyers smell sexism all the time." At one point, he demanded, "Your brains work differently. Maybe you're not as good in math. Why sue me because of that?"

USEFUL EXPLANATIONS

If Stossel's special seemed familiar, it's because its big scoop—Science Proves Sex Differences Are Inborn!—is a perennial favorite of the media. It was a *Time* magazine cover story, "Sizing Up the Sexes," in 1992 (1/20/92); shortly after Stossel's program aired, *Newsweek's* cover (3/27/95) featured "The New Science of the Brain: Why Men and Women Think Differently."

But Stossel's program came at an opportune time: With affirmative action up for review on Capitol Hill, *Boys and Girls Are Dif-*

ferent handily advances the arguments against such policies. "Biologically identifying traits of oppressed groups is always for the purpose of justifying the oppression," says Peter Breggin, psychiatrist and author of *The War Against Children*. "The thrust behind such research is a social policy, to keep people in their place and reinforce the status quo."

Throughout history, science has been used to explain and justify women's place. In the 19th Century, women's supposed lesser intelligence was explained by their smaller brains. Today, as Carol Tavris points out in *The Mismeasurement of Woman*, instead of weighing brains, scientists are dissecting them.

If, as EXTRA! has reported (1/2/95), the media "let *The Bell Curve*'s pseudoscience define the agenda on race," John Stossel's selective science tried to set the agenda on gender. By claiming to have science on his side and dismissing his critics as ideologues and censors, Stossel can present his socio-economic agenda as a natural law. As Fausto-Sterling told EXTRA!, "They could have called the show 'John Stossel's One-Hour Editorial.' Just don't call it news."

| "Hormones . . . have profound effects on just about every organ in the body."

HORMONES DETERMINE GENDER TRAITS

Dorion Sagan

In the following viewpoint, Dorion Sagan argues that men and women have numerous biological differences that manifest in various gender traits. According to Sagan, research has shown that hormones are the source of these gender differences. These hormones influence virtually every organ in the body, determining how men and women will react to diseases and drugs. Sagan is the co-author of *What Is Sex?* and *Origins of Sex: Four Billion Years of Genetic Recombination.*

As you read, consider the following questions:

1. Why are strokes sometimes less debilitating for women, according to Sagan?
2. In the author's view, why does cardiovascular disease affect women later in life?
3. What have been the cultural effects of body size, in Sagan's opinion?

Reprinted from Dorion Sagan, "Gender Specifics: Why Women Aren't Men," *The New York Times*, June 21, 1998, by permission of the author.

Western thought about sex—from the story of Eve to Aristotle's belief that girl babies arise from cooler sperm—has been tainted by the notion that the female is a kind of imperfect or unfinished male. Medical science, however, has gone from treating women as though they were simply smaller men to realizing that sex confers many more differences than those that are related to reproduction.

In contrast to the feminist premise that women can do anything men can do, science is demonstrating that women can do some things better, that they have many biological and cognitive advantages over men. Then again, there are some things that women don't do as well.

DIFFERENCES IN THE BRAIN

One of the less visible, but theoretically very important differences, is the larger size of the connector in women between the two hemispheres of the brain. This means that women's hemispheres are less specialized: a stroke that damages the left side of the brain leaves men barely capable of speech, while the same damage to a woman's brain is far less debilitating since she can use both sides for language. Although there is no hard evidence, the larger connector may also account for a woman's tendency to exhibit greater intuition (the separate brain halves are more integrated) and a man's generally stronger right-handed throwing skills (controlled by a left hemisphere without distractions).

Mary Catherine Bateson, the cultural anthropologist and a former president of Amherst College, has described women as "peripheral visionaries" able to follow several trains of thought (or children) simultaneously. Men, by contrast, seem more capable of focusing intensely on single topics. Our strengths, then, come from our differences rather than from our similarities.

Science and medicine are finally realizing that the differences that exist between men and women necessitate developing distinct therapeutic treatments addressing the specifics of our physiology. For example, doctors like Dr. Susan G. Kornstein, at the Medical College of Virginia's department of psychiatry, are advocating the use of sex-specific assessment and treatment of psychiatric disorders, like depression.

SEX-SPECIFIC TREATMENT

In a paper published in the Journal of Clinical Psychiatry, Dr. Kornstein points out that while depressed men seem to respond best to drugs that affect two neurotransmitter systems, those involving norepinephrine and serotonin, women respond better to drugs that affect only the serotonin system.

These differences in the therapeutic benefits of drugs not only underscore the need for medicine to go beyond giving women tapered doses of whatever is being prescribed for men (a latter-day offshoot of the women-as-incomplete-men theory), but support the idea that men's and women's brains do not function the same way.

Indeed, it is not only our brain functions that apparently diverge, but just about every aspect of our physiology. The way we metabolize alcohol and drugs, the way our circulatory system works and how resistant we are to infection are all affected by our sex.

HORMONES ARE CENTRAL

Why? Hormones.

In utero, girls and boys are chromosomally different; one might wag that the determinant of maleness, the Y chromosome, named for its shape, is "missing" something that the female determinant, the X chromosome, has. But they look identical. The development of characteristic male and female sexual genitalia at birth and of secondary sexual characteristics like breasts during adolescence, result from influxes of hormones, including estrogen and testosterone.

But the hormones we once thought were important only for pregnancy, lactation and sexual drive have profound effects on just about every organ in the body. In fact, the reproductive organs, which from a biologist's perspective are our only reason for existing, control and contribute to everything from mood to how cholesterol is used in the body.

Assigning such an important role to the reproductive organs is not new to our belief system. In ancient Greece, women who were classified as having nervous or "hysterical" disorders were thought to be suffering from an upward dislocation of the womb. Treatment for nervousness and hysteria entailed, among other things, trying to repel the womb back into place by applying noxious-smelling odors to the mouth and nose.

As a few women can testify today, the perception that the reproductive organs caused hysteria later manifested itself in the widespread use of hysterectomies and ovarectomies to treat behavioral disorders among American women during the early part of this century.

Science and medicine have historically used biologically-based sex differences to justify obvious acts of misogyny. It is not surprising, then, that a natural response has been for women to insist on equality implicitly based on the assumption that the sexes are essentially the same.

Men and Women Have Different Health Problems

But women may be just as ill served by a medical profession that treats men and women as equals as by one that follows what Dr. Rudolf Virchow, a famous 19th-century German doctor, believed. (He was the first to describe leukemia and is regarded as the founder of cellular pathology.) As Dr. Virchow put it, "Woman is a pair of ovaries with a human being attached, whereas man is a human being furnished with a pair of testes."

Research demonstrates that while men begin to suffer from coronary artery disease earlier in life than women do, women are more likely to die of coronary complications once they are afflicted. Men are also more prone throughout most of their lives to high blood pressure, but as women get older, this advantage disappears.

A Growing Dialogue About Biology

Daily newspapers purvey information about behavior involving definitive brain images of sex differences in human cortical function. More importantly, there is now a sophisticated body of work that knits together the biological and social sciences. And there is every reason to expect that the expansion of the explanatory power of biosociology will continue. Developments in Darwinian medicine, neurophysiology, paleoanthropology, economics, and political science, and a host of other disciplines will continue to help sketch a picture of Homo sapiens rooted in nature, in history, and—critically—in prehistory. It is no longer heartstopping to discuss human biology in the academic community, while among feminists there is at last a potentially productive dialogue between those who still regard all sex differences as social constructs and those prepared to see them as embedded in the nature of humanity.

Lionel Tiger, *Wilson Quarterly*, Winter 1996.

The delayed onset of cardiovascular disease in women may be linked to the fact that the female hormone, estrogen, which is produced mostly by the ovaries, protects the circulatory system from disease. Differences in the quantities of estrogen, essential for organization and maintenance of tissues and organs in both sexes, plays an important role in brain development and appears to be the reason that men's brains are bigger, but women's brains have more neurons.

Estrogen makes blood vessels more elastic, stimulates them to expand and allow good blood flow, and prevents cholesterol accumulation on the inside of blood vessels. As women age, however, they lose the protective benefits of estrogen because, in a rather dramatic fashion, their bodies stop producing it.

LESS EFFECTIVE TREATMENTS

At the same time, some treatments that are used to prevent cardiovascular disorders—aspirin, for example—are less effective in women. Reporting in an issue of the *International Journal of Fertility and Women's Medicine*, Dr. Marianne Legato, of the Columbia University College of Physicians and Surgeons, notes: "Although aspirin use is associated with less frequent myocardial infarction in both men and women, it does not decrease the risk of stroke in hypertensive women, as it does in men."

There are a number of naturally produced compounds that fluctuate more in women than in men: steroids, for example, which are infamous on the street for their simultaneous role in developing muscles and shortening tempers.

It turns out that steroids, a class of compounds that includes sex hormones, may play an important role in the mood swings of menstruators. These hormones directly affect brain cells. The neuroactive steroid allopregnanolone, made from progesterone, dampens the sensitivity of brain cells; it works like benzodiazepine drugs, most familiarly Valium. When the progesterone level is high, a woman is calmer. When it is low, she may feel more anxious and irritable. Moreover, women with PMS become insensitive to the calming effects of Valium-like drugs.

There is a growing consensus that these steroids produced by the sex organs are responsible for the greater incidence of mood disorders and depression in women. And a growing body of research is pointing to a role for other, similar steroids in memory, stress and alcohol abuse.

In keeping with the increasing recognition that some powerful mind-altering substances are internally produced by hormones, it is no wonder that adolescence is often a time of emotional turbulence. You cannot "Just say no" to your body's own genetically timed release of mood-altering sex hormones at puberty.

DRUGS AND GENDER DIFFERENCES

What society considers "recreational" drug use, which often begins at adolescence, may sometimes be motivated by an effort to self-medicate, changing or reversing the effects of sex hormones and neuroactive steroids. The notorious mood swings of adolescents may very likely reflect the body's adjustment to new concentrations and combinations of these compounds.

Lester Grinspoon, an associate professor of psychiatry at Harvard Medical School and an advocate of the medical use of marijuana, points out that marijuana has long been known as a palliative for the psychophysical pains of menstruation. Queen Victoria, according to her doctor J.R. Reynolds, used it for that purpose. Curiously (and although since disputed), one of the few medical studies on marijuana suggests that its use lowers testosterone levels in men.

Perhaps this drug, among others, interacts with or works in a similar way to the hormonal and neuroactive steroids. In any case women, who are twice as prone as men to depression, and who have a higher body-fat-to-muscle ratio and more hormonally distinct brains cannot be expected to respond to drugs, legal or illegal, in the same way men do.

The sexual distinction that biology traces to chromosomes and hormones also applies to culture and language. I recall, for example, being put in the girls' group at a day camp as a child because my first name was assumed to be female.

EVOLUTIONARY EXPLANATIONS

Evolutionists believe that the first sexual reproducers were unisexual cells that became involved in cycles of merging and separating. The first fertilizations probably occurred among starving microbes that cannibalized, but did not completely devour each other, becoming instead two-in-one cells.

Sexual differences evolved gradually over hundreds of millions of years. With these differences came ways of recognizing them. In many species, including humans, the gametes, or sex cells, of the females became fewer, bigger and more sedentary while those of the males became smaller, more fast-moving and numerous. But in humans, while the female sex cells, or ova, are far larger than the male gametes, or sperm, full-grown men are bigger than full-grown women.

The cultural ramifications of body size have been considerable, including the virtual absence of rapes committed by women. They may also have influenced the development of greater female cunning and social acumen to mitigate four million years of male bullying.

In our patrilineal culture, the family name is usually that of the man. Biology tells a more matrilineal story: the tiny DNA-containing oxygen-using inclusions in all of our cells, called mitochondria, come solely from our mothers. Nonetheless, culture remains, for lack of a better term, male-dominated. The French psychoanalyst Jacques Lacan even argued that all speech is part of the "symbolic order"—the largely negative, male realm of language and rules that supplants the original affirmative closeness of mother and child.

SCIENTIFIC SEXISM

The psychologist Theodore Roszak, who has been exploring what he calls the "twisted sexual politics of modern science," argues that science insidiously reinforces a partial male perspective. "Hard" sciences, like physics and chemistry, Mr. Roszak contends, are venerated, while "softer" sciences, like anthropology and psychology, are disparaged.

"Macho science," he argues, leads to bizarre fictions like selfish genes and cannibal galaxies. Female perspectives, he says, offer science new balance and openness.

From sex among equal single cells to male feminists offering cultural critiques of science's rhetoric, we have learned that the two sexes, subtly different, develop differently, respond differently to certain drugs and see the world in different ways. As the French say, vivé la difference.

| "While many people seem to fit one
of two sexes, do not discount the
many intersexual people."

THE IDEA OF MULTIPLE GENDERS IS NECESSARY

Alex Gino

Society needs to accept the notion that not everyone fits neatly into one of the two commonly accepted gender categories, argues Alex Gino in the following viewpoint. Gino contends that many people, such as transsexuals and cross-dressers, behave in ways that are more typical of the opposite sex. In addition, Gino asserts, intersexual people fall in between the two categories. Gino argues that people should not be forced into a category and should be able to live as they choose. At the time this viewpoint was written Gino was a senior at the University of Pennsylvania.

As you read, consider the following questions:

1. According to the author, what is the difference between sex and gender?
2. How many intersexed children are born each day in the United States, according to Gino?
3. In the author's view, how are those people who cannot be classified by gender viewed?

Reprinted from Alex Gino, "What Doesn't Fit in the Boxes," *Daily Pennsylvanian*, September 24, 1998, by permission.

Often, the words "sex" and "gender" are mistakenly used synonymously in our society. This usage, however, is erroneous. Sex refers to the biological characteristics of a person, whereas gender refers to what society imposes onto a person based on their sex.

For example, breasts fall under the category of sex, while wearing bras is a product of gender.

A Problematic Belief

Another faulty belief common in our society is that there is a one-to-one correspondence between sex and gender. Most people categorize their fellow human beings by distinguishing, "Men have penises and women have vaginas." There are several problems with this dichotomy.

As humans, it's natural to want to classify people to begin making sense of our surroundings. But when people do not easily fit within someone's "identification boxes," the identifier does not know what to make of the situation. Particularly in the cases of sex and gender, many demand that all people fit into one of two boxes: "Male" or "female." No in between, no bit of each.

What about transgender people—people who don't easily fit either of these categories.

For instance, transsexual people are people who have either undergone or will undergo sex reassignment surgery to become a member of the opposite socially accepted sex from the one they were assigned at birth.

There are also intersexual people, who were born with or later developed ambiguous genitalia. Usually, these people undergo involuntary surgery to "fix" themselves. Often they express a wish that they could have been raised as themselves, not as a "boy" or a "girl."

Medical operations to force children to fit into one sex category often leave a person with little or no sensitivity in the genital area. Losing the ability to achieve an orgasm in order to achieve social acceptance? It doesn't seem right to me.

Different Categories

Another group of people who are difficult to fit into binary categories are androgynous people, who consider themselves to lie somewhere in the middle of the male-female spectrum—or perhaps not in it at all.

And still another group are cross-dressers, a majority of whom are heterosexual men and feel more comfortable in clothing reserved for the other socially approved gender. Drag queens and drag kings love the camp value of dressing as the extremes of the other gender in their culture.

Imagine two points in space. Imagine a large number of dots on and near those points. As you move away from the points, the number of dots decreases. The end result is two overlapping circular sets of dots.

This is gender. Some people fit the point of "male" closely. Others fit the point of "female" closely. However, many do not. Many are in between or off to the side. These people are in no way less important or less equal than anybody else.

But there are only two genders, right? Or two sexes, or whatever?

More than Two Genders

Not quite. While many people seem to fit one of two sexes, do not discount the many intersexual people (approximately 20 such children are born daily in the United States).

At the central point of our imagined figure is the beautiful, perfectly proportioned, healthy, fertile, heterosexual, athletic, white, Anglo-Saxon person. Losing a breast to cancer makes a woman feel like "less of a woman." East Asian women are often eroticized as objects, not people. An infertile man is "not a real man" and "wimpy" men "throw like a girl."

Anything which causes society to see you as a less perfect version of your gender pulls you away from the central point.

A False Belief

One thing that mainstream patriarchal culture has in common with some brands of feminism and some gay politics is the insistence that there are only two genders—male and female. This is questionable on several levels.

Genetically it's clearly false: XX and XY aren't the only genetic combinations. Biologically it's clearly false: all human genitals grow from the same cells of the embryo, and there's a spectrum of possible development between what we call "male" and what we call "female".

Socially, we usually try to divide people into exactly two categories, even when they don't exactly fit them. Because so much of our society, even our language, is divided along gender lines, it's uncomfortable not to know what category someone belongs in. You wouldn't know what pronoun to use or what prejudices to hold about them.

Jennifer Moore, Outright, May 1997.

Some people choose to identify with that point in space. That is fine. Others do not. That should be fine as well.

Unfortunately, society does not see it that way. Remember Pat from *Saturday Night Live*? A perfect example. Someone who cannot be classified by gender is considered as disgusting, untouchable.

Often, seeing a person whose gender or sex is ambiguous, people will say, "I wish they'd just pick one." Why should people have to? You may choose to, but why must everyone fit into a little box? It may make your life easier to sort, but it won't reflect reality.

Life is complex. People are complex. Let them be who they are.

As someone who identifies as an androgynous, transgender, bisexual person, (or, as I prefer to say, a bi-trans-dyke sleeping with a man), I can say from personal experience that it hurts when people call me "miss." I don't want to be "sir." I just want to be a person. I hate that I am only given two choices on forms, "male" or "female."

"Which?" I want to ask. By sex, I'm female. By gender? Well, that's more complex. If the form is important, I'll put what people think. If it's not though, I get to write what I want.

"Sex: _____". . . "Yes please."

"M or F?". . . "No."

| "The division of the sexes is not a 'social construct.' It's a divine creation."

THE IDEA OF MULTIPLE GENDERS IS WRONG

Chuck Colson

In the following viewpoint, Chuck Colson contends that people who claim sexuality is a continuum and intersexuality is a legitimate gender category are incorrect. According to Colson, hermaphroditism is a deformity that should not be used to support claims for broadening the definition of gender. He argues that there are only two sexes and that God created those sexes. Colson is the founder and chairman of Prison Fellowship Ministries, a Virginia-based counseling program that operates in over 600 prisons throughout the United States.

As you read, consider the following questions:

1. What usually happens to babies afflicted with hermaphroditism, according to Colson?
2. In the author's view, what would happen to the Defense of Marriage Act if sexuality were a vast continuum?
3. In Colson's opinion, how do Christians determine normality?

Reprinted from Chuck Colson, "How Many Sexes Are There?" BreakPoint, 1996, by permission of Prison Fellowship Ministries, PO Box 17500, Washington, DC 20041-0500.

I magine you're wandering through a shopping mall, searching for a restroom. Suddenly you come across three doors: The first is marked "men," the second is labeled "women"—and the third door is marked "intersexual."

If the homosexual lobby has its way, this may become more than a bizarre fantasy.

Gay activists and their allies in academia are promoting the idea that human sexuality is not divided into distinct categories. They say that sexuality is a continuum, with people falling all along a spectrum. Support for this claim is supposedly found in a medical condition called hermaphroditism.

DIFFERING VIEWS OF HERMAPHRODITISM

Hermaphrodites are people born with both male and female sexual characteristics. Babies afflicted with this deformity usually undergo plastic surgery and hormone therapy, which enables them to function as either a male or a female.

But today a vocal lobby is contending that hermaphroditism is perfectly normal—that it's our attitude that needs fixing.

For example, in a journal called *The Sciences*, Anne Fausto-Sterling, a developmental geneticist at Brown University, says that hermaphroditism is proof that nature intended gender to be, in her words, "a vast, infinitely malleable continuum." In fact, she claims that humans come in at least five sexes, "including three types of intersexuals with varying degrees of male or female characteristics."

Morgan Holmes, a hermaphrodite who has never been surgically treated, supports this view. In a journal called *Queer Frontiers*, Holmes says that the traditional belief that people come in just two sexes, is merely a "social construct." Holmes is campaigning for a new gender category: "intersexual" or "transgender."

SEXUALITY AND IDEOLOGY

The idea that sexuality is a continuum has been standard dogma among sexologists since the work of Alfred Kinsey in the 1940s. The difference today is that the unfortunate victims of sexual deformities are being dragged in as biological proof of Kinsey's theory—ultimately for ideological purposes.

For example, Congress has passed the Defense of Marriage Act, or DOMA. The law was passed to forestall the possibility that Hawaii might force all 50 states to recognize same-sex marriage. DOMA limits marriage to unions between people of the opposite sex. But if sexologists are right, then there isn't an opposite sex—only a vast continuum from male to female, and

Reprinted by permission of Chuck Asay and Creators Syndicate.

everything in between. DOMA could not be sustained.

This illustrates the problem of taking biology as the baseline for behavior. The Bible teaches that the Fall into sin affected biology itself—that nature is now marred and distorted from its original perfection. This truth gives us a basis for fighting evil, for working to alleviate disease and deformity—including helping those unfortunate children born with genital deformities.

GOD DETERMINES GENDER

The non-Christian biologist has no standard but nature as it exists today. But for the Christian, nature is not our basis for determining normality. Scripture tells us how God created us before the Fall, and how He intended us to live: as males and females, reflecting His own image. We take our standards and identity from His revelation of our original nature.

The division of the sexes is not a "social construct." It's a divine creation. And that means all we'll ever need is two kinds of restrooms: one for men and one for women.

PERIODICAL BIBLIOGRAPHY

The following articles have been selected to supplement the diverse views presented in this chapter. Addresses are provided for periodicals not indexed in the *Readers' Guide to Periodical Literature*, the *Alternative Press Index*, the *Social Sciences Index*, or the *Index to Legal Periodicals and Books*.

Natalie Angier	"Men, Women, Sex and Darwin," *New York Times Magazine*, February 21, 1999.
Sharon Begley	"Gray Matters," *Newsweek*, March 27, 1995.
Mona Charen	"It May Not Be Destiny, But . . . ," *Women's Quarterly*, Spring 1998. Available from P.O. Box 3058, Arlington, VA 22203-0058
Alice Domurat Dreger	"A History of Intersexuality: From the Age of Gonads to the Age of Consent," *Journal of Clinical Ethics*, Winter 1998. Available from 107 E. Church St., Frederick, MD 21701.
Barbara Ehrenreich	"The Real Truth About the Female," *Time*, March 8, 1999.
Steven Goldberg	"Is Patriarchy Inevitable?" *National Review*, November 11, 1996.
Linda R. Hirshman	"Iron John and Shrinking Violet: Sex Education in the Columns of the *New York Times*," *Tikkun*, July/August 1995.
Gina Kolata	"Men and Women Use Brain Differently, Study Discovers," *New York Times*, February 16, 1995.
Irving Kristol	"Sex Trumps Gender," *Wall Street Journal*, March 6, 1996.
Harvey Mansfield	"Why a Woman Can't Be More Like a Man," *Wall Street Journal*, November 3, 1997.
Katha Pollitt	"Why Boys Don't Play with Dolls," *New York Times Magazine*, October 8, 1995.
Reed Edwin Pyeritz	"Sex: What We Make of It," *JAMA*, January 28, 1998. Available from 515 N. State St., Chicago, IL 60610.
John Schwartz	"Making Love, Not War," *Washington Post National Weekly Edition*, July 21–28, 1997. Available from 1150 15th St. NW, Washington, DC 20071.
Leora Tanenbaum	"Gene Tools," *In These Times*, February 6–19, 1995.
Deborah Tannen	"And Rarely the Twain Shall Meet," *Washington Post National Weekly Edition*, January 9–15, 1995.
John Taylor	"The Third Sex," *Esquire*, April 1995.

CHAPTER 2

HAVE WOMEN'S ROLES CHANGED FOR THE BETTER?

CHAPTER PREFACE

In early 1999, speculation arose over the political futures of a Clinton and a Dole. Not Bill Clinton and Bob Dole, the opponents in the 1996 presidential election, but their wives, Hillary and Elizabeth. Many political analysts were touting Hillary Rodham Clinton as a leading candidate for the New York Senate seat held by the retiring Daniel Patrick Moynihan, while observers also viewed Elizabeth Dole as a promising choice for the Republican presidential nomination in 2000. As of April 1999, neither woman had declared her candidacy. Elizabeth Dole did take a key step in March 1999 by forming an exploratory committee in order to begin fund-raising, making it more likely she would run for the presidency. While no official declarations have been made, the fact that they are seen as desirable candidates for two of the nation's most prestigious jobs is an indication that women have strengthened their political roles.

However, despite the speculation over Hillary Rodham Clinton and Elizabeth Dole, women have not yet achieved full equality at the higher levels of politics. While women are 52% of the population, there are only nine women in the Senate, 58 women in the House of Representatives and three women in governor's mansions. However, some states have come closer to equality. California has two women senators. In 1998, Arizona made history by becoming the first state to elect women as governor, secretary of state, treasurer, attorney general, and superintendent of public instruction. Although no woman has been president, popular opinion suggests such a scenario could come true. A poll by the White House Project, a public-awareness campaign to help people learn about women who could potentially run for president, shows that 76 percent of Americans are ready to elect a woman president. If Elizabeth Dole chooses to run for the presidency, and wins, the United States would face the unique situation of a former presidential candidate becoming the nation's First Husband.

Women still have a long way to go before their political power can be considered equal to men. In the following chapter, the authors debate the role of women in various arenas, such as work and family life, and whether their roles have changed for the better.

1

"It is a dangerous thing to assume that just because we were raised in a feminist era, we are safe."

WOMEN ARE STILL OPPRESSED

Ellen Neuborne

In the following viewpoint, Ellen Neuborne argues that women still face sexual inequality and must take steps to point out the sexism that affects their lives. Citing personal experiences, she contends the oppression is so pervasive that even feminists are programmed to accept the sexual biases found throughout society. Neuborne asserts that sexism is especially pervasive in the workplace, where women with young children are often treated as liabilities. She maintains that women, especially the younger generation of feminists, need to speak out against this oppression. Neuborne is an editor at *Business Week*.

As you read, consider the following questions:

1. According to Neuborne, what message has been sent by sexist programming?
2. In the author's view, what dangers do women pose to other women?
3. What message is Neuborne trying to send?

Reprinted from Ellen Neuborne, "Imagine My Surprise," in *Listen Up: Voices from the Next Feminist Generation*, edited by Barbara Findlen. Copyright ©1995 by Barbara Findlen. Reprinted by permission of Seal Press, Seattle, Washington.

When my editor called me into his office and told me to shut the door, I was braced to argue. I made a mental note to stand my ground.

It was behind the closed door of his office that I realized I'd been programmed by the sexists.

We argued about the handling of one of my stories. He told me not to criticize him. I continued to disagree. That's when it happened.

He stood up, walked to where I was sitting. He completely filled my field of vision. He said, "Lower your voice when you speak to me."

And I did.

I still can't believe it.

The Power of Sexist Programming

This was not supposed to happen to me. I am the child of professional feminists. My father is a civil rights lawyer. My mother heads the NOW Legal Defense and Education Fund. She sues sexists for a living. I was raised on a pure, unadulterated feminist ethic.

That didn't help.

Looking back on the moment, I should have said, "Step back out of my face and we'll continue this discussion like humans."

I didn't.

I said, "Sorry."

Sorry!

I had no idea twenty-some years of feminist upbringing would fail me at that moment. Understand, it is not his actions I am criticizing; it is mine. He was a bully. But the response was my own. A man confronted me. My sexist programming kicked in. I backed off. I said, "Sorry."

I don't understand where the programming began. I had been taught that girls could do anything boys could do. Equality of the sexes was an unimpeachable truth. Before that day in the editor's office, if you'd asked me how I might handle such a confrontation, I never would have said, "I'd apologize."

I'm a good feminist. I would never apologize for having a different opinion.

But I did.

Recognizing the Pattern

Programming. It is the subtle work of an unequal world that even the best of feminist parenting couldn't overcome. It is the force that sneaks up on us even as we think that we are getting ahead with the best of the guys. I would never have believed in its existence. But having heard it, amazingly, escape from my own mouth, I am starting to recognize its pattern.

When you are told you are causing trouble, and you regret having raised conflict, that's your programming.

When you keep silent, though you know the answer—programming.

When you do not take credit for your success, or you suggest that your part in it was really minimal—programming.

When a man tells you to lower your voice, and you do, and you apologize—programming.

The message of this programming is unrelentingly clear: Keep quiet.

I am a daughter of the movement. How did I fall for this?

I thought the battle had been won. I thought that sexism was a remote experience, like the Depression. Gloria [Steinem] had taken care of all that in the seventies.

Imagine my surprise.

And while I was blissfully unaware, the perpetrators were getting smarter.

NEW METHODS OF SEXISM

What my mother taught me to look for—pats on the butt, honey, sweetie, cupcake, make me some coffee—are not the methods of choice for today's sexists. Those were just the fringes of what they were really up to. Sadly, enough of them have figured out how to mouth the words of equality while still behaving like pigs. They're harder to spot.

At my first newspaper job in Vermont, I covered my city's effort to collect food and money to help a southern town ravaged by a hurricane. I covered the story from the early fund-raising efforts right up to the day before I was to ride with the aid caravan down South. At that point I was taken off the story and it was reassigned to a male reporter. (It wasn't even his beat; he covered education.) It would be too long a drive for me, I was told. I wouldn't get enough sleep to do the story.

He may as well have said "beauty rest." But I didn't get it. At least not right away. He seemed, in voice and manner, to be concerned about me. It worked. A man got the big story. And I got to stay home. It was a classic example of a woman being kept out of a plum project "for her own good," yet while in the newsroom, hearing this explanation about sleep and long drives, I sat there nodding.

Do you think you would do better? Do you think you would

recognize sexism at work immediately?

Are you sure?

WOMEN ARE STILL VULNERABLE

Programming is a powerful thing. It makes you lazy. It makes you vulnerable. And until you can recognize that it's there, it works for the opposition. It makes you lower your voice.

It is a dangerous thing to assume that just because we were raised in a feminist era, we are safe. We are not. They are still after us.

And it is equally dangerous for our mothers to assume that because we are children of the movement, we are equipped to stand our ground. In many cases, we are unarmed.

The old battle strategies aren't enough, largely because the opposition is using new weaponry. The man in my office who made a nuisance of himself by asking me out repeatedly did so through the computer messaging system. Discreet. Subtle. No one to see him being a pig. Following me around would have been obvious. This way, he looked perfectly normal, and I constantly had to delete his overtures from my E-mail files. Mom couldn't have warned me about E-mail.

WOMEN OPPRESS WOMEN

Then there is the danger from other women. Those at the top who don't mentor other women because if they made it on their own, so should subsequent generations. Women who say there is just one "woman's slot" at the top power level, and to get there you must kill off your female competition. Women who maintain a conspiracy of silence, refusing to speak up when they witness or even experience sexism, for fear of reprisals. These are dangers from within our ranks. When I went to work, I assumed other women were my allies.

Again, imagine my surprise.

I once warned a newly hired secretary that her boss had a history of discrimination against young women. She seemed intensely interested in the conversation at the time. Apparently as soon as I walked away, she repeated the entire conversation to her boss. My heart was in the right place. But my brain was not. Because, as I learned that day, sisterhood does not pay the bills. For younger women who think they do not need the feminist movement to get ahead, sisterhood is the first sentiment to fall by the wayside. In a world that looks safe, where men say all the right things and office policies have all the right words, who needs sisterhood?

We do. More than we ever have. Because they are smooth, be-cause they are our bosses and control our careers, because they are hoping we will kill each other off so they won't have to bother. Because of all the subtle sexism that you hardly notice until it has already hit you. That is why you need the movement.

FURTHER EXAMPLES OF INEQUALITY

On days when you think the battle is over, the cause has been won, look around you to see what women today still face. The examples are out there.

On college campuses, there is a new game called rodeo. A man takes a woman back to his room, initiates sexual intercourse, and then a group of his friends barges in. The object of this game is for the man to keep his date pinned as long as possible.

Men are still afraid of smart women. When Ruth Bader Gins-burg was nominated to the Supreme Court, the *New York Times* de-scribed her as "a woman who handled her intelligence grace-fully." The message: If you're smarter than the men around you, be sure to keep your voice down. Wouldn't want to be consid-ered ungraceful.

⌐WOMEN ARE NOT FREE

Unlike her male counterparts, the chief judge pours her own coffee, and the police officer may not use what she's learned on the job to stop her husband from beating her; whatever she's learned at work can't over-ride what she's learned all her life about being a woman. The female employee—not her male counterpart—is still expected to buy the gifts, take the coats, bake the cookies for an office party, babysit her employer's child. Hardly gang-rape, but sexism nevertheless.

Yes, the world is different now than it was when I was your age. In only thirty years, a visionary feminism has managed to seri-ously challenge, if not transform, world consciousness. . . . But the truth is women are still far from free. We're not even within striking range.

Phyllis Chesler, *Letters to a Young Feminist*, 1997.

A friend from high school calls to tell me he's getting married. He's found the perfect girl. She's bright, she's funny and she's willing to take his last name. That makes them less likely to get di-vorced, he maintains. "She's showing me she's not holding out."

In offices, women with babies are easy targets. I've seen the pattern played out over and over. One woman I know put in ten years with the company, but once she returned from maternity leave, she was marked. Every attempt to leave on time to pick up her baby at day care was chalked up as a "productivity problem." Every request to work part-time was deemed troublemaking. I sat just a few desks away. I witnessed her arguments. I heard the editors gossip when she was absent. One Monday we came into work and her desk had been cleaned out.

Another woman closer to my age also wanted to work part-time after the birth of her son. She was told that was unacceptable. She quit. There was no announcement. No good-bye party. No card for everyone in the office to sign. The week she disappeared from the office, we had a party for a man who was leaving to take a new job. We also were asked to contribute to a gift fund for another man who had already quit for a job in the Clinton administration.

But for the women with babies who disappeared, nothing happened. And when I talked about the fact that women with babies tended to vanish, I was hauled into my boss' office for a reeducation session. He spent twenty minutes telling me what a great feminist he was and that if I ever thought differently, I should leave the company. No question about the message there: Shut up.

FACING DOWN SEXISM

I used to believe that my feminist politics would make me strong. I thought strong thoughts. I held strong beliefs. I thought that would protect me. But all it did was make me aware of how badly I slipped when I lowered my voice and apologized for having a divergent opinion. For all my right thinking, I did not fight back. But I have learned something. I've learned it takes practice to be a strong feminist. It's not an instinct you can draw on at will—no matter how equality-minded your upbringing. It needs exercise. You have to think to know your own mind. You have to battle to work in today's workplace. It was nice to grow up thinking this was an equal world. But it's not.

I have learned to listen for the sound of my programming. I listen carefully for the Sorrys, the You're rights. Are they deserved? Or did I offer them up without thinking, as though I had been programmed? Have you? Are you sure?

I have changed my ways. I am louder and quicker to point out sexism when I see it. And it's amazing what you can see when you are not hiding behind the warm, fuzzy glow of past feminist victories. It does not make me popular in the office. It does not even make me popular with women. Plenty of my female colleagues would prefer I quit rocking the boat. One read a draft of this essay and suggested I change the phrase "fight back" to "stand my ground" in order to "send a better message."

But after falling for the smooth talk and after hearing programmed acquiescence spew from my mouth, I know what message I am trying to send: Raise your voice. And I am sending it as much to myself as to anyone else.

NEW GOALS FOR FEMINISM

I've changed what I want from the women's movement. I used to think it was for political theory, for bigger goals that didn't include my daily life. When I was growing up, the rhetoric we heard involved the theory of equality: Were men and women really equal? Were there biological differences that made men superior? Could women overcome their stigma as "the weaker sex"? Was a woman's place really in the home?

These were ideas. Important, ground-breaking, mind-changing debates. But the feminism I was raised on was very cerebral. It forced a world full of people to change the way they think about women. I want more than their minds. I want to see them do it.

The theory of equality has been well fought for by our mothers. Now let's talk about how to talk, how to work, how to fight sexism here on the ground, in our lives. All the offices I have worked in have lovely, right-thinking policy statements. But the theory doesn't necessarily translate into action. I'm ready to take up that part of the battle.

THE NEXT GENERATION OF FEMINISM

I know that sitting on the sidelines will not get me what I want from my movement. And it is mine. Younger feminists have long felt we needed to be invited to our mothers' party. But don't be fooled into thinking that feminism is old-fashioned. The movement is ours and we need it.

I am one of the oldest of my generation, so lovingly dubbed "X" by a disdainful media. To my peers, and to the women who follow after me, I warn you that your programming is intact. Your politics may be staunchly feminist, but they will not protect you if you are passive.

Listen for the attacks. They are quiet. They are subtle.

And listen for the jerk who will tell you to lower your voice. Tell him to get used to the noise. The next generation is coming.

| "Women want and need to celebrate
how far they've come."

WOMEN ARE NOT OPPRESSED

Elinor Burkett

In the following viewpoint, Elinor Burkett argues that the goals of women's liberation have been largely achieved. She contends that women's opportunities in education and the workplace have increased dramatically since the 1960s. Burkett asserts that feminists need to celebrate this success and focus on the problems that do affect women, such as caring for children and aging parents. Burkett is the author of *The Right Women: A Journey Through the Heart of Conservative America*, the book from which this viewpoint is taken.

As you read, consider the following questions:

1. In the author's view, who is the heroine to American women in the late 1990s?
2. How are antifeminist women actually living up to feminist ideals, according to Burkett?
3. Why can the feminist movement not be stolen, in Burkett's view?

Somehow during the past twenty-five years, feminism—as a movement, rather than as a set of ideals—has managed to alienate itself from its own constituency, and after I'd interviewed women for two years, the reasons became pretty clear. American women have real problems that wrack their lives—bread-and-butter issues, the tension between work and family, worries about aging parents and fears about growing children—and the National Organization for Women spends its time suing Hooters. Women's lives are intimately entwined with those of their fathers and sons and husbands, and feminists preach the kind of identity politics that separates women from men. American women want—need, in fact—to have fun, and they have fun by dressing up and making up and flirting; but too many feminists worry about Ms. magazine's announcing that it is okay for women to pluck their eyebrows and mock women who dream of silky underwear from Victoria's Secret.

IGNORING REALITY

Leaders of the women's movement gather at expositions and symposia and sing the praises of the strength and invincibility of women, then appear on the nightly news bemoaning women as weak victims. They proclaim that women can, and should, have it all, forgetting that most women are so tired, so worn out, so burdened with responsibility that the very thought of having it all is enough to engender 5 million simultaneous nervous breakdowns. They broadcast anger—for them, a delicious, exhilarating emotion—when all most American women want is a free hour to sit and enjoy Roseanne joking about being a "domestic goddess" instead of a housewife, who figures she's done her job if the kids are still alive at 5 P.M.

After all, in the late 1990s, it is Roseanne, not Gloria Steinem, who is a heroine to American women—no matter what the New York Times and its allied publications might think. Their ideological and spiritual guru isn't Susan Faludi or Patricia Ireland, but Oprah Winfrey, who offers them guidance on losing weight rather than lectures on fat as a feminist issue.

Feminism has discredited itself with American women because it is so intent on theory that it loses touch with reality. Women's lives are messy composites of work and relationships, responsibilities, dreams and desires that don't fit neatly into theoretical straitjackets. It's easy to create a theoretical framework that proves sisterhood across class and race lines, but few black women in urban ghettos experience solidarity with the suburban matrons whose toilets they clean. It's intellectually interesting to demonstrate how the patriarchy oppresses women and gives advantage to anyone with a penis, but such theory does little to explain Margaret Thatcher, or the shabby life of the homeless man. It's theoretically consistent to argue that men and women are natural antagonists, but such antagonism gives heterosexual women little comfort when they're lonely or sick or aging.

And when women's lives refuse to fit into these ideological superstructures created on university campuses, feminism's theoreticians don't reconsider the superstructures. They set themselves up as ideology cops and demand that women reconsider their lives. But American women have achieved enough empowerment—to use the overworked word of the nineties—to rebel against those demands, and to treat that new police force with that peculiar admixture of contempt and dismissal Americans reserve for most self-styled authority figures.

Furthermore, while feminism has convinced many men that women deserve to win the Oppression Sweepstakes, the movement has convinced fewer women, who know that their husbands have miserable jobs, that they too live in terror of being laid off. The gender card doesn't work among those who refuse to be straitjacketed by gender, and women have learned enough from feminism to shrug off any externally imposed straitjackets, no matter who is imposing them.

THE IMPACT OF WOMEN'S LIBERATION

Ultimately, American women have rejected the feminist movement not merely because it has become the home of humorless carpers, but because they sense that the movement doesn't really like or respect women—not just the fantasy of women, not just women who follow the movement's leaders like lockstep Nazis, but that broad range of people of the female persuasion who inhabit American womanhood. The movement holds women to impossibly high, and absurdly narrow, standards and gives them no credit for being able to forge their own separate peace, treating them precisely as disapproving men have been wont to do. It disparages their choices and demeans their intelligence by bemoaning most of their decisions as still further evidence that they are victims of backlash.

In a world heavy with uncertainty, confusion and outright fear, women want and need to celebrate how far they've come, even as they need tax credits and safe streets and better math classes for their children. The last thing they want, or need, is the added burden of being asked to die on the front lines in a war they believe has been largely won.

For even while women reject feminism, the movement, they have embraced the fundamental ideals of women's liberation more thoroughly than even the most idealistic feminist of the 1960s could have imagined. Equal pay for equal work, equal educational opportunity, respect and pride—demands that seemed like dreams less than three decades ago—are assumptions, not to mention the law, in most of the land. American women know that paradise has yet to be achieved, but they also know with full certainty that they don't live in the world of their mothers, for better and for worse. They no longer have to confine their job searches to the employment section for women in their daily newspapers. They no longer have to worry that their daughters won't be admitted to graduate school in math or physics. When American women refuse to characterize themselves as feminists, they are rejecting the terminology, not the activity, because they don't like the company they'd be keeping if they put themselves in the former category. . . .

THE CHANGING VIEWS OF AMERICAN WOMEN

The reality of the evolving thinking among American women is undeniable, despite the repeated attempts of feminist leaders to indulge in contradictory fantasies. Time and time again—virtually ad nauseam—I hear young women [saying]: "I don't want to be a member of a group. I wasn't raised by a group; I was raised by a family. I resent the notion that I have to owe my success to something beyond myself." I regularly listen to women of all ages repeating the sentiments of Blanquita Cullum, a conservative Hispanic radio talk show host in Washington, D.C.: "Feminists want to neuter me. I'm sick of their worrying about the lower half of my body. Tying me to the lower half of my body is like tying me to the kitchen." And I have come to understand that the bitter disappointment of Jenny Westberg [a prolife feminist] is shared by thousands of women who tried, and failed, to find a place in the feminist movement. "At some point, apparently, the feminist establishment determined that they needed a great deal fewer adherents, and began systematically excommunicating one another for violating a standard of Total Philosophical Purity. Excluded (or highly suspect) groups include: prolifers; Republicans; Libertarians; conservative Democrats; members of most organized religions; stay-at-home mothers/wives; and anyone who dissents from whatever unwritten agenda is currently in force."

So the issue is no longer whether this emerging reality is an accurate reflection of women's thinking, or how it arose, but what this reality—a reality which cuts across class, race, regional and generational lines—means for American women and their politics. Dismissing it by bemoaning American women as victims of backlash, as the dupes of misogynists and a brainwashing, antifeminist media is tempting, but doing so creates a feminist nightmare, rife with contempt for women's intelligence and integrity, reeking of the sort of blithe dismissiveness with which men have traditionally treated women. And while theories about quasi-conspiracies by media, industry and political leaders against women's advancement might be deliciously fun to contemplate, ultimately, conspiracy theories are like hot fudge sundaes—not all that good for you. The time might still be ripe in America for countering unpleasant truths by casting aspersions on the sincerity and social consciousness of the truth makers. But shooting the messenger does not kill the message, or the fact that neither side in women's debates has a monopoly on integrity.

Feminism Has Succeeded

After spending two years talking to American women, I have come to realize that feminists need not bemoan, distance themselves or even wrack their brains trying to figure out how to reverse this new reality, for the rising visibility of conservative women and the mounting rebellion against the feminist movement are not signs that feminism has gone astray, as many conservative pundits, and many women, suggest. Rather, they are the clearest possible evidence that feminism has been successful, so successful that women no longer need to cling to one another in the type of solidarity which is inevitably a reflection of oppression. After all, even the most committed self-styled conservatives aren't pawns of powerful men trying to send women back into the kitchen. In fact, despite their antifeminist rhetoric, they are living up to the highest feminist ideals by seizing control over their own lives, by refusing to be confined or manipulated by anyone else's definitions of who or what they should be, by examining the choices open to them and following their own hearts and minds in selecting their path.

The initial dismay and confusion about the state of American women's politics which provoked my journey has, in fact, gradually transmogrified into pride in American women, conservative and otherwise. Sisters are doing it for themselves. After years of struggle and anguish, we don't yet have nirvana, but women finally have enough power and forbearance to splinter in a thousand directions, and still succeed. We no longer need to agree about the nature of marriage and the role of the family in reinforcing the patriarchy; women's options are now so broad that we need not speak in one voice to be heard. We no longer have to feel threatened by women who rejoice in the sacrifices of motherhood; that choice poses no threat to those of us for whom sacrifice does not connote nobility. We no longer need to worry about whether women are genetically different from men; men are no longer the gold standard against which humankind is judged. And we no longer need to fight over who owns feminism. The victory belongs to all of us: to Christian women who are running for political offices that they could never have aspired to thirty years ago, to young women who can't imagine a world without opportunity, to Republicans, Libertarians and Democrats.

Feminism's most prolific critics, women like Elizabeth Fox-Genovese and Christina Hoff Sommers, have a vested interest in blinding themselves to these overarching changes. They are poised to build their careers on declarations about how feminism is not the story of their lives, or how the movement has been stolen by dastardly demagogues with whom they disagree. But that's just malarkey. Feminism is the story of the life of every woman in the nation, whether she acknowledges it or not, and the movement can't be stolen because it is ubiquitous, residing in every household that includes a woman, in every business forced to comply with the law and on every television station that broadcasts *Roseanne* and *Murphy Brown* and *Chicago Hope*.

Younger Women Have Rejected Feminism

Younger women, in their twenties, are not buying the feminist package. They are marrying earlier, and generally seem unimpressed with the politics and the work-life balance embraced by the boomers. These younger women don't accept that there is ideological content to the fact of a career, or that feminism owns women's professional achievements. They appear to go to law school and get married without much angst.

Lisa Schiffren, *Crisis*, April 1995.

And all too many feminists similarly recoil from these changes, from embracing the diversity of lifestyle, political opinion and faith that has sprung from their own efforts because they refuse to own anything, or anyone, not dressed in the right outfit—or perhaps because admitting that you have been ousted from the center stage of history is simply too painful. But the truth is that without anyone realizing it, feminism got away from them; it broke loose from the feminist movement and began to grow wild across the land. Adapting itself to a dozen different soils and climates, it has mutated often into something barely recognizable. But its roots are strong and it energizes women wherever they live, work, pray and play. Feminism—not gender feminism or power feminism or any of the other self-serving subgroupings that are antithetical to the spirit of a movement that is, by definition, all-embracing— has become part of the fabric of American life. It's as American, and as diverse, as apple pie.

Rewriting Feminism

Signs of victory are everywhere: on the pages of the want ads of every newspaper in the country and in the gender of the commentators on the nightly news, on the basketball court and the assembly lines in Detroit, at the winners' circle of the Iditarod, the installations of female college presidents and the launchings of tens of thousands of women-owned businesses. American women aren't talking about feminism. They aren't writing about it, theorizing about it or marching for it. They're just doing it. Women's rejection of feminism, the official movement, should not be a cause for dismay. It should be a cause for celebration. American women are rewriting feminism, and, in the rewriting, they have made it their own.

| "However you slice and dice the numbers . . . women earn less than men, except in a few rare instances."

WOMEN FACE DISCRIMINATION IN THE WORKPLACE

Katha Pollitt

In the following viewpoint, Katha Pollitt asserts that statistics suggesting women have made progress in closing the wage gap are misleading, contending that women, especially mothers, continue to be discriminated against in the workplace. Pollitt argues that the purported shrinking income gap does not take into account the fact that women with children suffer economically, while men with children do not. According to Pollitt, women continue to experience wage discrimination because typical female jobs often offer little advancement or are not adaptable to the needs of working mothers. Pollitt is an associate editor for the *Nation*.

As you read, consider the following questions:

1. Why are the earnings of young men and young women comparable, according to Pollitt?
2. According to the author, what would women's earnings be relative to men's, if male wages had remained at their 1979 levels?
3. Why do women start their own businesses, in Pollitt's view?

Reprinted from Katha Pollitt, "Go Figure," *The Nation*, April 14, 1997, by permission of the publisher.

Why is it that some women are always trying to persuade other women that their troubles are grossly exaggerated? A few years ago we were told that date rape was really "bad sex" and domestic violence a much-overblown—and genderless—problem. More recently, the word was that the barriers to equal participation in electoral politics are down—it's women's lack of confidence and interest that keeps Congress 90 percent male. Now comes the Independent Women's Forum (who else?) under the aegis of the American Enterprise Institute (who else?) to argue that job discrimination against women is a thing of the past, and that statistics and studies indicating otherwise are an attempt to promote "victim status for women."

FALSE FIGURES

"Women's Figures" (note the cutesy pun) by Diana Furchtgott-Roth and Christine Stolba is an elegant little booklet—thick, creamy paper, brightly colored graphs, lots of airy white space between the lines, a three-page bibliography and many quotations from I.W.F.'s own Elizabeth Fox-Genovese. It comes with a shiny blue bookmark listing all the A.E.I. phone numbers and home-page address, and it fits right into your purse. Unfortunately it's full of half-truths, non sequiturs, advocacy numbers, unproven assumptions and buried premises—but then, how could it not be, given that what it argues is insane?

According to Furchtgott-Roth, depressing statistics about sticky floors, glass ceilings and women's earnings vis-à-vis those of men—71 cents on the male dollar, up from 59.4 cents in 1970—give a false picture of women's current prospects: Only in recent years have women had the access, education, consistent participation in the work force and, she suggests, desire to equal men in the job market. To assess the effect of economic discrimination today we need to look at young women, and if we do we find that "National Longitudinal Study of Youth data show that among people ages 27 to 33 who have never had a child, women's earnings approach 98 percent of men's earnings." Thus, with a wave of a statistical wand, a 29-cent wage gap shrinks to a 2-cent wage gap. Do you think Furchtgott-Roth could come over and do my taxes?

What's wrong with this statistic? Well, in the first place, young men and women have always had earnings more comparable than those of their elders: Starting salaries are generally low, and do not accurately reflect the advantages that accrue, or fail to accrue, over time as men advance and women stay in place, or as women in mostly female kinds of jobs reach the end of characteristically short career paths. In the second place, the figure applies only to the childless, but by age 33, 76 percent of women are mothers. And, as Heidi Hartmann of the Institute for Women's Policy Research explained to me, childless women and childless men are different: Since children negatively affect women's careers, but have either no effect or a positive effect on men's, young women without children tend to be those most dedicated to their professional advancement, whereas young men without children are more likely to be (I'm just quoting here) misfits. Furchtgott-Roth's simple little statistic turns out to be a veritable gift basket of apples and oranges.

BALANCING MOTHERHOOD AND WORK

For Furchtgott-Roth, what looks like discrimination is really the result of women's personal choices. Women choose to have children, and make work choices that fit in with domesticity: jobs with fewer demands, flexible hours and that require skills that don't deteriorate over time. (This points to one of those contradictions in right-wing ideology I love so much: Motherhood is simultaneously the very definition of women's existence—rejection of which has caused the country to go to pot—and a free, individual choice, like buying a motorcycle, whose costs the individ-

A WIDENING WAGE GAP

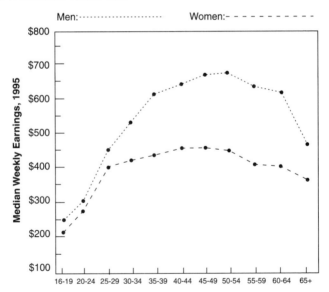

Men:·········· Women:- - - - - - - - - -

Unpublished tabulations, Bureau of Labor Statistics, Current Population Survey.

ual must bear alone. I guess if women decided not to bear those costs humanity would just die out.) One might ask why only mothers bear the costs of children, and why Furchtgott-Roth doesn't include money as one of the things working mothers want out of their work. One might also note that some of the biggest mostly female job categories are famously inflexible (nursing) and require constantly updated skills (anything involving computers), and that the 29-cent wage gap concerns full-time workers, not part-timers on the "mommy track." Besides, childless women also earn less than men as time goes on. But beyond that, why isn't the resistance of the job market and the workplace to working mothers' needs an aspect of economic discrimination against women?

"Women's Figures" makes much of the progress women have made in closing the wage gap, but it does not mention that most of that gain is a statistical artifact produced by stagnant or declining male wages. If men's annual earnings had remained at their 1979 levels, women in 1995 would have earned only 63 cents on the male dollar. Not a lot of progress for sixteen years. Similarly, "Women's Figures" trumpets the growth and success of women's businesses, while failing to mention that one of the reasons women start their own businesses is that they get fed up with being discriminated against in the corporate world, and that most women-owned businesses are small and precarious ventures. And what about the poor, who are disproportionately female? Furchtgott-Roth reprints the Cato Institute's discredited table claiming that welfare benefits add up to a pretty good salary: from a lavish $36,400 in Hawaii to a modest but tidy $11,500 in Mississippi. I wonder how Fox-Genovese, who only a few years ago was lambasting the women's movement for abandoning poor and minority women, likes them apples.

DISCRIMINATION PERSISTS

As economics, "Women's Figures" is claptrap. However you slice and dice the numbers—by age, education levels, across job categories or within them, women earn less than men, except in a few rare instances (acting in porn movies, for instance). But as ideology it's kind of interesting. Here we see the usefulness of anti-feminism to right-wing free-marketeers like the folks at the A.E.I.: Since remedying gender discrimination would require government and other sorts of intervention and regulation, wouldn't it be helpful if gender discrimination could be found not to exist? I choose, you choose, the corporations choose, the right-wing think tanks choose, we all choose together!

"The fuss about male discrimination against women in the marketplace is much ado about very little."

WOMEN DO NOT FACE DISCRIMINATION IN THE WORKPLACE

Lawrence W. Reed

Despite the claims of some critics, women do not face discrimination in the workplace, argues Lawrence W. Reed in the following viewpoint. He contends that statistics indicate women have made considerable gains in earning power and wield more power in the boardroom than they did in the past. According to Reed, women have made these advances by attaining college educations, not by relying on affirmative action programs. He asserts that any wage gap is not the result of discrimination but because women make different lifestyle choices from men, largely due to marriage and childbirth. Reed is the president of the Mackinac Center for Public Policy, a free-market research and educational organization.

As you read, consider the following questions:

1. In 1995, what percentage of bachelor's degrees was earned by women, according to statistics cited by Reed?
2. In the author's view, what would a person expect to see if women did face widespread discrimination by men in the marketplace?
3. According to Warren Farrell, as cited by Reed, how many hours a week do women work inside and outside the home?

Reprinted from Lawrence W. Reed, "Are Women Being Victimized by the Market?" *The Freeman*, April 1998, with permission from the publisher.

One of the many false but frequent criticisms of the marketplace is that it discriminates against women. It goes like this: if the market is fair, why do women own fewer businesses and earn less than men for doing the same work?

Groups organized for the purpose of getting government to intervene insist that women are victims of widespread discrimination in America, held down by the "glass ceiling" of male bias. They paint the market as a place where silly prejudices determine wages, where it actually pays for employers to exploit an entire gender of employees, where men conspire against businesses owned by females. These groups propose a range of harmful, redistributive pseudo-remedies: wage controls, compulsory quotas and affirmative-action schemes, daycare subsidies, and the like.

WOMEN HAVE SUCCEEDED IN THE MARKETPLACE

Economists have demolished this criticism in many venues (including *The Freeman*), but it comes up again and again. So again, here's a rebuttal.

In "Women's Figures: The Economic Progress of Women in America," published in 1996 by the American Enterprise Institute, Diana Furchtgott-Roth and Christine Stolba showed conclusively that the marketplace is working for women far better than its critics admit. For instance: when all factors, such as experience and life situations, are held constant, women between the ages of 27 and 33 earn 95 to 98 percent as much as the average male worker—a statistically insignificant difference.

More good news: from 1987 to 1992, the number of women-owned businesses in America rose by 43 percent. Today, women earn the majority of associate's, bachelor's, and master's degrees. Nearly 40 percent of doctorates are awarded to women. And during the past decade, the number of female executive vice presidents more than doubled and the number of female senior vice presidents increased by 75 percent.

EDUCATION IS THE KEY

Skeptics might be tempted to say that it wasn't women's efforts or the marketplace that explain these facts, but sex-based preference programs encouraged by government. Wrong again. An analysis by Sally Pipes and Michael Lynch in the Heritage Foundation's *Policy Review* debunked that myth, too. Pipes and Lynch proved that more women are going to college and that this is the primary reason for the significant advances in female earning power.

In 1960, for example, only 19 percent of bachelor's degrees were earned by women, but by 1995 women claimed a whopping 55 percent. Over the same period, women increased their share of lucrative professional degrees—MBAs, MDs, and JDs—by at least 500 percent. The increase in college enrollment is a result not of government-enforced preferences, but of changing cultural patterns and personal choices that enable women to excel in fields formerly dominated by men.

The so-called "wage gap" between men and women, say Pipes and Lynch, is due not to senseless discrimination. It's caused by statistical differences in age, education, and continuous years in the work force. Because women experience more interruptions in their working careers than do men—usually because of marriage or childbearing—the wages they can command in the market are slightly discounted. That is not unfair; indeed, it is perfectly rational economic behavior on the part of employers concerned about their bottom lines.

WOMEN MAKE DIFFERENT CHOICES

It is personal choices in education and career that explains largely the gaps and changes in women's wages and work status. . . . We don't need to expand affirmative action for women.

First, let's agree that as a group and on average, women do earn less than men at all educational achievement levels. But let's also look at the fields the majority of women choose to study.

Arguments like these are fuzzy without numbers, so consider an example. In 1992, 75% of masters and Ph.D.'s conferred in education went to women. In that year, 86% of masters and Ph.D.'s earned in engineering went to men. Now the average monthly wage for an advanced education degree holder is $3,048, while for an advanced engineering degree holder is $4,049. Compare the two and, as they say here in Las Vegas: Bingo. You get a wage gap of $1,001. However, the actual wage difference is because of personal choices. On average, education jobs pay less than engineering jobs and that explains the gap.

Susan Au Allen, *Vital Speeches of the Day*, April 1, 1997.

The *Detroit News* (April 25, 1996) showed that what differences exist between the wages of men and women are largely a consequence of lifestyle choices: "According to the U.S. Census, men on average spend 1.6 percent of their work years away from the job; women are away 14.7 percent. Ten years of seniority raises wages more than 25 percent, according to government figures. [Former] Labor Secretary Robert Reich may opine that women are 'unable' to build seniority, but men are 'unable' to give birth."

"Nor is there evidence," says the *News*, "that biology is destiny. Women hold triple the percentage of top management jobs compared with similarly 'seasoned' males. And 81 percent of Fortune 500 boards feature women directors; a third of the companies have more than one. Women also own 7.7 million businesses, employing 15.5 million workers—a third more than employed by Fortune 500s."

NO WIDESPREAD DISCRIMINATION

If there were widespread or substantial discrimination against women by men in the marketplace, then one would expect to see *female* employers paying their female employees more than *male* employers pay their female employees for the same work. Not so. No evidence. Zip.

No one should deny that some men, even some male employers, discriminate against women in ways that cannot be explained by lifestyle choices or impersonal market forces. The point is, most are smart enough not to because they understand that it's self-defeating. Pay a woman less than she's worth and you hand a golden money-making opportunity to a competitor.

A fascinating 1994 book, *The Myth of Male Power*, takes the charge of male discrimination against women and turns it on its head. It is encyclopedic in its presentation of previously unpublished facts and figures. The author, San Diego writer and consultant Warren Farrell, is more than qualified to address the subject: he is a former three-time elected male board member of the nation's foremost radical feminist outfit, the National Organization for Women.

MEN AND WORK

Farrell says that men account for 94 percent of the occupational fatalities each year. Undoubtedly that stems from the fact that men make up more than 95 percent of the work force in hazardous occupations.

Though men enjoyed virtually the same life expectancy as women as recently as 1920, they now live an average of seven years less. Female longevity has soared almost 50 percent in the past 70 years.

Women do more housework than men, but men do more workplace work. On average, men labor an average of 61 hours a week (counting work inside and outside the home), while the figure for women is 56, says Farrell. His conclusion: if men are oppressing women, it sure doesn't show up in the numbers.

In the end, the fuss about male discrimination against women in the marketplace is much ado about very little, with a lot of carelessly unexplained figures tossed about that, in any event, hardly argue for government to coercively interfere with privately arranged contracts and relationships between consenting adults.

"This country cannot go to war without women on the front lines."

WOMEN'S OPPORTUNITIES IN THE MILITARY NEED TO BE EXPANDED

Rosemary Mariner

In the following viewpoint, Rosemary Mariner argues that women's opportunities in the military should be expanded to include combat roles. She asserts that women make important contributions to America's defense and should be treated like their male counterparts. Mariner maintains that the military risks lowering its standards if it restricts the opportunities of its female volunteers and places less-qualified men in combat positions. Mariner is a naval aviator and the first woman to command an aviation squadron.

As you read, consider the following questions:

1. According to Mariner, what are the only two combat positions in which women cannot serve?
2. What percentage of America's military force is female, as cited by the author?
3. In Mariner's view, what is the only alternative to allowing women equal opportunities in the military?

Reprinted from Rosemary Mariner, "Can't Go to War Without Women on Front Lines," *The Washington Post*, May 11, 1997, with the permission of the author.

In 1973, when I joined the Navy, going into the military was one of the most politically incorrect things a young person could do. At the end of the Vietnam War, my decision to become a Navy pilot made me a "baby killer" in the eyes of many college classmates. Twenty-four years later, in the wake of the Army's sexual misconduct scandals, and the highly publicized troubles of Air Force Lt. Kelly Flinn, I am again pilloried for wearing the uniform of my country—this time because I am a woman.

MILITARY MYTHS AND REALITIES

In the twisted commentary surrounding the Aberdeen misconduct cases, one might get the impression that female soldiers are just problems, forced into uniform by radical feminists who strike terror in the heart of combat-hardened generals. In this fantasy world, military men are animal-like warriors, able to control weapons of mass destruction but not their sexual urges. Anyone who doesn't agree with this view is "politically correct." In a force of 1.5 million people, the solution to a dozen married middle-age sergeants abusing privates in advanced vocational schools is to segregate female trainees. The very legitimacy of military women is being questioned.

In American military tradition, we do not rape, plunder or pillage enemy combatants, let alone fellow soldiers. To suggest that wearing a uniform is an excuse for adultery or assault is an insult to the overwhelming majority of honorable military men and women. That is no less true for Lt. Flinn than for her male counterparts.

That such nonsense is publicly debated underscores a general ignorance of the realities of military service and women's service in particular. Before any serious discussion of sexual misconduct in the military can take place, a reality check is needed.

Contrary to culture war propaganda, women serve in the armed forces because they directly contribute to our central mission, national defense. Integrating large numbers of high-quality female recruits into nontraditional fields made the all-volunteer force possible. As a result of the Persian Gulf War, women serve in all combat positions except those classified as "direct ground combat" and aboard submarines. Desert Storm demonstrated that combat exclusion policies do not protect women from coming home in body bags or becoming POWs. Rather, such arbitrary restrictions hurt combat readiness by limiting the flexibility of commanders to use all their soldiers, however needed, especially under fire. In terms of plain fairness, if American women are good enough to die for their country, they are good enough to fight.

SEGREGATION IS WRONG

The entire history of women in the military, including two world wars, has been a steady progression away from all-female auxiliaries toward full integration. Not only do we train as we fight, but segregating any force is the antithesis of unit cohesion, inherently unequal and violates unity of command. As with racial separation, the idea of keeping people "with their own kind" has nothing to do with combat readiness or stopping harassment. The purpose of Jim or Jane Crow policies is to keep an institutionally inferior group in its place.

The vast majority of American men do not want to be in the military, let alone in combat positions. In 1998 the armed forces must enlist more bright young people than ever to replace those leaving active duty. If women were forced into an ancillary role, the Defense Department would have to significantly increase the number of lower mental category men and high school dropouts. Even if force structure is dramatically cut, the declining pool of eligible youth does not alter the demographic imperative. In the age of "dominant battle space maneuver" where brains are more important than brawn, the nation would be faced with the absurd prospect of conscripting unmotivated men to replace quality female volunteers.

WOMEN ARE CAPABLE

In terms of the demands of infantry warfare, women have proved themselves capable of fighting under even the most arduous of conditions. Whether the women of the Gulf War, those who served with me in the Marines, or women police officers I know who are fighting crime today on America's meanest streets, American women have clearly demonstrated ample dedication, stamina and just plain guts.

Timothy C. Brown, *Wall Street Journal*, September 30, 1997.

Today, with almost 15 percent of the total force female, including women warriors, ours is the most combat-ready peacetime force in history. Military women are not a social experiment but an integral part of the armed forces. They, like men, must be judged as individuals. Public defamation of active duty personnel is in itself divisive and hurts readiness by pitting soldier against soldier. Internally, the military must resolve the outstanding issues of gender integration. Externally, we dare not squander our success by pandering to a few vocal critics pushing an anti-woman social agenda at the expense of national security. No amount of nostalgia over manly warriors protecting fair maidens erases the fact that this country cannot go to war without women on the front lines.

No Turning Back

The post-Vietnam War military I joined had lost the confidence of the American people. Through determined leadership and a professional all-volunteer force, we earned back the nation's respect. But if the armed forces fail to deal with our current problems, we again risk breaking faith with a public unwilling to voluntarily serve in an institution that practices denial. Either women serve honorably and equally, or we draft men. Turning back the clock on gender integration means a return to the broken force of the early 1970s. Those of us who served then, know there is no going back.

| "The arguments for women in combat positions are riddled with double standards."

WOMEN'S OPPORTUNITIES IN THE MILITARY DO NOT NEED TO BE EXPANDED

Suzanne Fields

In the following viewpoint, *Washington Times* columnist Suzanne Fields argues that women's opportunities in the military should not be expanded to include combat roles. She asserts that arguments supporting women in combat are inconsistent and rely on double standards. Fields contends that feminists want female soldiers to be seen as too weak to stand up to male superiors who harass them but strong enough to battle enemies. According to Fields, expanding women's military opportunities will exacerbate sexual harassment and abuse and will create a less efficient military.

As you read, consider the following questions:

1. According to Fields, what is the inconsistent logic in the radical feminist argument supporting women in combat?
2. In the author's view, what are armies not designed to do?
3. What proposition should those who support women in combat make, according to Fields?

Reprinted from Suzanne Fields, "Warriors or Damsels in Distress?" *The Washington Times*, May 19, 1997, with the permission of the publisher.

To hear the feminists tell it, America couldn't win a war without regiments of women in combat boots. The "social experiment" was a success.

WOMEN ARE NOT NEEDED IN COMBAT

But that yokes together two different propositions. Women may be essential to the operation of the armed services, but not for combat. Putting them in a fight for their lives is definitely a "social experiment."

Typically, the woman-in-combat-on-air-sea-and-land-defense is made by Capt. Rosemary Mariner, the first woman to command an aviation squadron. She scorns the argument against women in combat as "anti-woman," the intellectual equivalent of treating women as damsels in distress.

"Externally, we dare not squander our success by pandering to a few vocal critics pushing an anti-woman social agenda at the expense of national security," she writes in The Washington Post. "No amount of nostalgia over manly warriors protecting fair maidens erases the fact that this country cannot go to war without women on the front lines."

If that were true, and it isn't, we have no combat-ready forces, since women are still barred from ground combat. Women can take over all kinds of military jobs to free men who are combat-ready without facing combat themselves. The arguments for women in combat positions are riddled with double standards.

DOUBLE STANDARDS IN THE MILITARY

A woman soldier may not be a "fair maiden," but she can certainly hide behind her vulnerability. Women who cry harassment in the armed services are drawing more on the damsel-in-distress scenario than picturing themselves as robust combatants. If a woman soldier can't kick a male soldier where it hurts when he attacks her sexually, how can we expect her to protect herself—and her buddies—against an enemy soldier?

There is an inconsistent and contradictory logic at the root of this radical feminist argument, which extends far beyond the culture of the military. One is that men are bad, but a woman can be as bad as any man. Another is that a man can take advantage of a woman in and out of the military by seeking sexual favors, and the woman will oblige because she's afraid not to. (The reverse of this sexual scenario doesn't exist.)

In deciding whether men should train women or women should be trained by members of their own sex, the focus ought to be on the fundamental biological difference between men and women: Aggressive men can quickly become aggressive sexually and women who barter their sexuality for favors will let them get away with it. This is not "blaming the victim." It's acknowledging the reality in the war between the sexes. Instead of a director exploiting his power over the ingenue on the casting couch, male trainers exploit a female recruit's vulnerability in the boot-camp barracks.

NOT A SOCIAL EXPERIMENT

Men can be disciplined to control their appetites, but an army is designed to fight wars, not conduct sociological experiments. Common sense dictates that efficiency should be the name of the military's game, and women are far less likely to harass and abuse women than men are.

The crusading feminist motto was once that "fathers can mother." An eminent sociologist of the era wrote that, well, yes, that is probably true, but we would have to invest an incredible amount of time, energy and money (training programs) to turn men into the same kinds of nurturers that women are, and they would be likely to backslide without women watching over them with eternal vigilance.

Reprinted by permission of Chuck Asay and Creators Syndicate.

Most men can control their sexual appetites without taking advantage of women, but in the volatile atmosphere of Army life, men who are given power over female recruits require a vigilance and discipline that the Army has so far failed to achieve.

COSTS TO THE NATION

When military efficiency must account for sexual relations (and offenses) as well as pregnancies, astute men and women should ask themselves how much the nation is willing to pay for a "social experiment" rejected by the rest of the civilized world.

If the women who yearn to be warriors were serious, they might make this proposition to their critics: "Let's organize women into all-female combat units, and we'll show you we're the equal of men." Feminists are outraged by the suggestion because they can't imagine women going into battle without men at their side. Men, on the other hand, have been going into battle without women for centuries.

"Motherhood is viewed as a sucker's game."

SOCIETY HAS LOST ITS RESPECT FOR MOTHERS

Marian Kester Coombs

In the following viewpoint, Marian Kester Coombs contends that society is declining because motherhood is no longer respected, especially by women. She argues that motherhood was once viewed as a valuable role for women and served as a way to humanize children. However, Coombs maintains, modern feminism now wants to destroy femininity and motherhood in order to make women as masculine, if not more so, than men. She asserts that the result of this feminist movement will be a violent, cynical, and pagan society. Coombs is a freelance writer for the *Washington Times* and *Chronicles*.

As you read, consider the following questions:

1. How does the author define masculism?
2. In Coombs's view, how do many girls escape the regendering program?
3. What does the author find most unsettling about modern youth?

Reprinted from Marian Kester Coombs, "Estrogen Poisoning," *Chronicles*, May 1997, with permission. *Chronicles* is a magazine of American culture; a publication of The Rockford Institute, 928 N. Main St., Rockford IL 61103.

A first-grade teacher in the suburbs of Washington, D.C., con-
cludes that while some of her pupils suffer various degrees
of parental neglect, others seem to be experiencing the opposite
extreme: such pampering at home that they cannot even tie
their own shoes, and must have it done for them. It takes a
while before she realizes that the latter children cannot tie their
shoes because no one has ever taken the trouble to teach them.

INDIFFERENT PARENTING

A developmental psychologist at the University of Rochester is
disturbed by the high rate—13 percent and rising—of "attention-
deficient," "hyperactive" six- to twelve-year-old boys being dosed
with Ritalin in that urban area. After reporting on her informal
observation of several mother-son pairs ("Son cuddled next to
Mom. Son ran the strings from the hood of Mom's jacket through
his lips. Son rocked his body back and forth. Son patted Mom's
face. Through all of this, Mom ignored him"), the psychologist
writes, "What's behind the alarmingly high incidence of [Atten-
tion-Deficit Hyperactivity Disorder] ADHD, I believe, is the widespread failure of parents and teachers to help children learn to
regulate themselves, including managing their attention. Many
parents do not seem inclined to socialize their children."

A young working mother is having a dreadful time finding
someone, *anyone* to whose mercenary mercies she can safely en-
trust her precious two-year-old, and so she writes an angry little
get-it-off-my-chest piece for *Woman's Day.* "Day care in America is
such a hodgepodge, antiquated affair that parents are forced to
take a leap of faith with the well-being of their child that they
wouldn't take with any other part of their lives," she whines.
"We are so vulnerable. . . . Where is the affordable, decent day
care that will let parents go off to work secure in the knowledge
that their child is being well cared for? . . . Does it really have to
be this gut-wrenching?" By now we do not have to be told what
such whining precedes: still another demand for still another fix
of big government.

When *The Awakening* was published in 1899, public reaction
to author Kate Chopin's hostility toward those lowly creatures
she termed "mother-women" was disbelief that any woman
could feel that way about motherhood, and scandalization at
the sheer "perversity of her unnatural sentiments." A mere
three generations later, Ms. Chopin's sentiments have been almost universally adopted by our society—most fervently, in
fact, by mothers themselves.

Fatherlessness has been tagged as the biggest problem facing the family in this country today, and by extension the biggest problem facing our society as a whole. But it is really *motherlessness* that besets us. Nobody wants to be the mom. Motherhood is viewed as a sucker's game. Yet what a wondrous system it was, admirable in its lavish economy, its unimpeachable irrationality, its gloriously selfish selflessness, its universal particularity. Every child was to have at least one person on earth who was absolutely crazy about him, a sucker for him. Every child was to be the diminutive king or queen of at least one person's susceptible heart. The usual law of life—*Eat or be eaten!*—did not apply to motherhood, which gloried, up till now, in giving—*Eat, eat!* But big-government feminism has decreed that motherhood must go; taxes are levied against it; studies are concocted to prove it baneful; and so it is going.

"Feminism" is a misleading term for the culprit, however. What these infuriated women want to do is get rid of femininity altogether, to seize and wield what they clearly consider to be superior, masculine attributes. The movement should rightly be called *masculism*; it is the triumph of all values traditionally associated with the male: dominance, aggression, egotism, single-mindedness, profanity, promiscuity, toughness, brutal objectivity, aloof self-sufficiency. Even the bodies of men—the sculpted musculature of flat abs and steel glutes—are displayed as templates for the new woman to reproduce herself upon. Not for her the female body as temple wherein the race is reproduced. Everything women have historically been associated with, among every people, in every land and age, is being devalued and derided in the name of "feminism."

With these acquired masculine characteristics, then, young women are to force themselves into the mold of citizen-soldier, power attorney, "extreme" all-out athlete. Arrayed in teams, sorted into rigid hierarchies, exhorted to "Go for it!" no matter who or what stands in their way, women are to become male impersonators. Not mere impersonators, of course: one of the central beliefs of masculism is that women are and have always been just as good (that is, as *masculine*) as men, and indeed will prove better at the game once they have taken it over. This belief was recently stroked by a Foundation for the Future study "proving" that females in the labor force are superior to males in 28 out of 31 ways.

True Masculinity Is Mocked

But "masculism" is also a misleading term. It is not really the masculinization but the *homosexualization* of society that is occurring. True masculinity is unswervingly attracted to the feminine; as Isak Dinesen, a female Nietzsche, wrote in her epigrammatic fashion, "The love of woman and womanliness is a masculine characteristic, and the love of man and manliness is a feminine characteristic. . . . [I]t is almost impossible for a woman to irritate a real man, and as to the women, a man is never quite contemptible, never altogether rejectable, as long as he remains a man." In contrast, it is the homosexual mind that finds both the truly feminine and the truly masculine—that is, the heterosexual—unspeakably distasteful. It is the true natures of both men and women that have been targeted for denunciation and destruction. Why? Because the traditional familial order of society is an immovable object in the path of the irresistible force of the state and its plans for our improvement.

A SOCIETY WITHOUT WISDOM

Time was when supporting mothering was mere common sense. Sometimes I think we live in an anti-wisdom society. The only Ideas that are Exciting challenge long-held beliefs. Evolutionists and journalists like [Joan K.] Peters frequently point to remote tribes to prove their points (Peters praises the Tahitians, who have no "gender differentiation" and are "thus" peaceful), throwing out 2,000 years of western civilization and its Judaeo-Christian emphasis on committed relationships and family. Pretty soon we will be questioning whether people even *need* significant others—why not a series of "mutually enhancing" relationships (it takes a village . . .)? Can you imagine anyone asserting that romantic love, with its desire to be with the beloved, is a "myth"? Yet that is what some are saying about the even more intense and emotional desire of a child to be with his mother.

Maria McFadden, *Human Life Review*, Spring 1998.

Thus at the same time masculine attributes are aped, their originators—men, and white men in particular—are savagely mocked and attacked for possessing or exercising them. The Virginia Military Institute's "rat line," a typically male institution for the breaking of young colts by stallions, is horrific if manned by males, but somehow terrific if populated by sweating, shorn, and swearing females. Men's-club or locker-room camaraderie is reprehensible, but the same behavior transposed to a female key is right on. Boys and men are ridiculed (and medicated) for having "testosterone poisoning," while women bulk up on steroids to win Olympic medals.

Now there are those who suspect that this massive female invasion of male turf is only a scheme hatched by levelers and pacifists to neuter men's warlike nature and thereby destroy "militarism" from within. And such may well be the case; certainly this is the aim of Patsy Schroeder and the next Chief Justice of the Supreme Court, Ruth Bader Ginsburg. Any wicked fairy tale can come true in the Age of Clinton.

Nevertheless, the female masses are not wise to the plot. They have bought and swallowed the regendering program whole. In high schools and colleges throughout the country, it is *verboten* for girls to admit they would like to be wives and mothers when they grow up. The only way to escape the program—and a way increasing numbers of desperate girls are taking—is to get pregnant and opt out of "higher education" altogether. For the rest, their lives as women will be, and in many cases already have been, sacrificed to the dizzyingly swift ongoing inversion of all values. Thus we get the grisly spectacle of women lobbying passionately for partial-birth abortions while understandably crazed men shoot up abortuaries. The former protected status of women as the more vulnerable sex will probably never recover. Women face the worst of both worlds: vulnerability and "equality."

THE THREAT OF MOTHERLESS CHILDREN

Daughters brought up motherless do not learn to be mothers. Motherless sons do not learn to respect or love women. Such denatured generations are swiftly arising to overtake us. The underclass, from which "welfare" has banished fathering, experiences little but mortally wounded mothering, while the former middle class, now thoroughly proletarianized, manages its own demoralization along convergent lines, slavishly conforming to the state's desire to turn all human activity into taxable wage labor. Particularly hard hit are young men, always more difficult to socialize in any case. Ironically, most high-achieving men have had mothers with strong, dominant personalities—precisely the sort of women least likely to have or stay home with children in the modern era. Hardest hit of all are young white men, whose precipitous drop from top of the heap to lowest of the low is surely the most spectacular sociopolitical descent in the annals of man.

What sort of world will motherless children make, these feckless youths and charmless maidens? An awful sullenness; a routine violence; an aggressive, gnawing sense of entitlement superimposed upon an even deeper conviction of worthlessness (euphemistically called "lack of self-esteem"); a cynical disbelief in any ideal, in anything noble or transcendent in the human project; a reductionist, materialist stupefaction unresponsive to beauty or truth; and in the midst of all this, a most superstitious credulity. The sudden wholesale return of pagan pantheism with its dream-catchers and fetishes and angel apparitions—hallucinations born of religious deprivation—gives new life to G.K. Chesterton's words: "When man no longer believes in God, he does not then believe in nothing, but in anything."

The unsettling thing about modern youth is their lack, not of manners, but of *souls*. Among the many practices that should distinguish human society from animal life, the most important is the quality and intensity of mothering, supported manfully by fathering. No other species invests more time and energy, more nurturing, more *love* in its offspring than humans do. And this pays off: the offspring are humanized. They develop that special, species-specific luxury, a soul. It is solely for the sake of that soul that human beings cherish one another. When it disappears, the self-conception that makes possible the human social world dies with it.

And so does God Himself. As [nineteenth-century German philosopher] Ludwig Feuerbach observed, our idea of God flows from the physical reality of the family, *die Heilige Familie*: father-judge, mother-nurturer, child-beloved. What will God become once bereft of the family? What He is already fast becoming: the criminally negligent but judgment-proof nanny state, jealously clutching its hoard of dead souls.

"If having children and grandchildren is so universally rewarding, why is it selfish to deny oneself the pleasure of parenthood?"

SOCIETY DOES NOT RESPECT CHILDLESS WOMEN

Joan Smith

In the following viewpoint, Joan Smith argues that women, such as herself, who have chosen not to have children are unfairly criticized by society. She asserts that society views childless women as bizarre and selfish and that childlessness is considered acceptable only if the woman is physically unable to have children or has chosen a religious career over heterosexual relations. She advocates that women should have the right to make different lifestyle choices without being punished. Smith is a journalist and the author of numerous novels and nonfiction works, including *Different for Girls: How Culture Creates Women*, from which this viewpoint is taken.

As you read, consider the following questions:

1. What are some of the reactions encountered by women who say they do not want to have children, according to the author?
2. According to Smith, what was the deciding factor in her choice to remain childless?
3. In addition to joining the cloister, how did St. Catherine escape motherhood, in Smith's view?

When an individual woman says she doesn't want to have children, she immediately encounters a spectrum of hostile reactions ranging from disbelief ('you'll change your mind when you're older') to condescension ('you don't know what you're missing'), from accusations of solipsism ('have you *always* been so selfish?') to full-frontal assaults on her femininity ('what's *wrong* with you?'). I can speak with some authority on this subject because I am one of those women; I have no idea whether I am fertile, sub-fertile or incapable of conceiving, for I have never been interested enough to find out. If I have a biological clock, it must be silent and digital, for I have never heard it tick, even though I am (at the time of writing) in my early forties. Over the years, however, I have become wearily familiar with all the responses outlined above, and with some bizarre variants such as 'How dare you not have children when other women are desperate to get pregnant?' Equally popular is a testy demand that I should lie about my reason for not having children, that I should hint at lengthy and unsuccessful courses of fertility treatment, thereby emphasising the point that childlessness is just about acceptable for a woman as long as it isn't voluntary. Obviously I could lower my eyes, take out a handkerchief and pretend that I'm resigned to my barren state. Or I could go along with the line of a well-meaning friend who said she admired my decision not to have children because it was one of the most difficult a woman could make. But it isn't, not for me. I grew up not wanting children in the same way that I didn't aspire to be an airline pilot or a nuclear physicist; there was no painful soul-searching or introspection, just a useful and early piece of self-knowledge I have always trusted and acted upon.

On its own, this lack of interest in having children might not have equipped me to withstand the astonishing degree of social pressure on women to conform to a single pattern. The deciding factor was knowing from an early age exactly what I did want, that I was absolutely impassioned about being a writer. It's not that I thought writing and motherhood were incompatible, just that having such a fierce ambition threw into shadow all the things—including having children—that I didn't want to do. I have never felt the need to apologise for this. I didn't enjoy being a child, a point I make when people accuse me of not realising what I'm missing; I was one for what seemed a maddeningly long time, about a third of my life so far, and leaving behind that infantile and adolescent world was a tremendous relief. I put away childish things gladly, to put my own gloss on St Paul, and I don't want to re-encounter them in surrogate form in the role of somebody else's parent. This is not to devalue motherhood, not for those who want to do it and who delight, as I don't, in the company of small children. What I do insist on is the right to be different without being punished or pitied, a right men take for granted.

HOSTILITY TOWARDS CHILDLESS WOMEN IS PERVASIVE

In case you think I'm exaggerating the hostility that women like myself routinely encounter, here is a piece of writing—it's actually a radio review from the *Independent*—which displays some of the reactions I've been talking about:

> The thing that people without children never seem to appreciate is the full-blooded, gutsy thrills involved in rearing the next generation. 'Without Issue', a feature on Radio 4 last night about why women choose not to have children, opened with a stereotypically cute little montage of childhood sounds—a tinkling musical box and a lisping voice reciting a nursery rhyme. . . .

> If infancy really was as icky as it sounded there, childlessness ought not to be so much an option as a legal obligation. But to have children is not to cut yourself off from the dirt and squalor and moral depravity of everyday life; it's to be thrust into a new world of primal emotion, of instinctive violence unconstrained by fear or scruple. One male interviewee on 'Without Issue' complained that parents he knew seemed to use children as an excuse not to do interesting and exciting things. The poor sap: sure, whitewater rafting may offer more of a physical challenge than putting a pair of dungarees on a protesting two-year-old; but it's unlikely to offer a more intense emotional experience. Children are a test of character more exacting than anything you're likely to encounter outside Homer.

> Speaking—as you've probably deduced—as a parent, I've always thought that not having children was a perfectly reasonable option. 'Without Issue' left me less sympathetic. Early on, one woman complained that people told her not having children was selfish, and Liz Lochhead, who linked the interviews with a polemical commentary, took her side: after a succession of interviewees talked about how they wanted their sleep, and wanted money, and didn't want the responsibility, she asked whether it would be kind for such people to have offspring.

> It's a fair point; all the same, it was hard not to be struck by the rampant individualism on display here—epitomised by Christina Dodwell, who talked about her ideal moments on top of a mountain with virtually no human life for miles. Perhaps they didn't realise it, but these people came across as devout Thatcherites, dedicated to the belief that there's no such thing as society.

An Illogical Debate

As it happens, I am the interviewee singled out by the author of the piece (a journalist named Robert Hanks) in his third paragraph. To demonstrate that Hanks is far from alone in his casual assumption of moral superiority over childless people, here is the final paragraph of a letter sent to the *Guardian* by a female reader who was incensed by an article I wrote about choosing not to have children:

> Just one thing—when my time comes to leave this world (not too far distant I guess) I'll look at my grandchildren and feel that I have done something to contribute to things. . . . Perhaps having written a few words on a word processor, paper, what have you, gives one the same feeling of achievement? I shall never know.

Articles and letters like the ones I've just quoted reveal the hopeless confusion which surrounds the subject of voluntary childlessness. If having children and grandchildren is so universally rewarding, why is it *selfish* to deny oneself the pleasure of parenthood? If, on the other hand, bringing up children is as arduous a task as Hanks suggests, why does he feel sorry for people who don't do it? But logic doesn't have much place in this debate—it's actually more of a slanging match, with most of the insults flying in one direction—because it very quickly becomes bogged down around this single issue of altruism. This is not surprising, given that the adulation of motherhood, especially as encouraged by the Christian churches, can be understood as a *quid pro quo* for undertaking what were, for most of

A Lack of Cultural Support

As I look back over the last couple of generations, I'm hard-pressed to find a cultural trend that offers any support for women who don't want to have children. My Baby Boomer, ex-hippie friends love to rail against the '50s stereotype of the perfect housewife, but their '60s counterculture movement simply reinforced the motherhood ideal from a new angle: Motherhood is natural, and therefore beautiful, like having sex or smoking grass. Now, in the alternative-consciousness or New Age movements of today, motherhood is promoted as a powerful spiritual path, aligning women with the "Great Mother" of us all. While I'm glad we've uncovered a mythology that does honor to the mothers among us, I wish that we could write that story without leaving women like me out in the cold.

Rose Solari, *Common Boundary*, September/October 1996.

recorded history, the dangerous activities of pregnancy and childbirth; even now, in Italy, the Catholic Church is considering the beatification of a woman who died after refusing cancer treatment which would endanger her unborn child. Until very recently, the only practical escape route for women who wished to avoid repeated pregnancies was the cloister; significantly, they were required to undertake an alternative form of altruistic surrender, giving up both the world and sexual pleasure. (St Catherine of Siena, according to historians, 'received visions which led her to vow her virginity to Jesus Christ' and in doing so escaped her mother's exhausting fate of producing more than twenty children. Catherine's persistent and well-documented anorexia, one of whose effects is to prevent menstruation, may have been another unconscious strategy to avoid motherhood. It is a striking fact that she shared the condition with other religious women of the period, most of them far less celebrated but equally resistant to self-nourishment and female maturity.) In other words, a woman who wanted to remain childless had to atone through another, very public act of self-denial. Those twentieth-century women like myself who choose not to have children, yet continue to enjoy sexual relations with men, fail on both counts.

PERIODICAL BIBLIOGRAPHY

The following articles have been selected to supplement the diverse views presented in this chapter. Addresses are provided for periodicals not indexed in the *Readers' Guide to Periodical Literature*, the *Alternative Press Index*, the *Social Sciences Index*, or the *Index to Legal Periodicals and Books*.

Ginia Bellafante   "Feminism: It's All About Me!" *Time,* June 29, 1998.

Charles S. Clark   "Feminism's Future," *CQ Researcher,* February 28, 1997. Available from 1414 22nd St. NW, Washington, DC 20037.

Diana Furchtgott-Roth and Christine Stolba   "American Women Aren't Really So Cheap," *Wall Street Journal,* November 20, 1998.

Al Gini   "Women in the Workplace," *Business and Society Review,* no. 99, 1998. Available from Blackwell Publishers, 350 Main St., Malden, MA 02148.

Glamour   "Why the U.S. Military Needs More Women," October 1997.

Steven A. Holmes   "Sitting Pretty: Is This What Women Want?" *New York Times,* December 15, 1996.

Wendy Kaminer   "Will Class Trump Gender?" *American Prospect,* November/December 1996.

Iris Krasnow   "Discovering Motherhood," *American Enterprise,* May/June 1998.

Katha Pollitt   "Dead Again?" *Nation,* July 13, 1998.

Elayne Rapping   "The Ladies Who Lynch," *On the Issues,* Spring 1996.

Carl Rowan   "Why We Must Break the 'Glass Ceiling,'" *Liberal Opinion,* February 10, 1997. Available from PO Box 880, Vinton, IA 52349-0880.

Jeanne Safer   "Childless by Choice," *New York Times,* January 17, 1996.

Christina Hoff Sommers   "Feminism Is Not the Story of Their Lives," *Heterodoxy,* May/June 1996. Available from Center for the Study of Popular Culture, PO Box 67398, Los Angeles, CA 90067.

Olivia Vlahos   "The Herstory of Warfare," *Women's Quarterly,* Autumn 1995. Available from PO Box 3058, Arlington, VA 22203-0058.

CHAPTER 3

HAVE MEN'S ROLES CHANGED FOR THE BETTER?

CHAPTER PREFACE

The term "single parent" is often synonymous with "single mother." In 1997, single women headed 9.86 million families, while only 1.86 million families were led by single fathers. However, that latter number has grown at a rate of 10 percent a year, while the percentages of two-parent and single-mother families have remained fairly constant. The increase of men taking on a traditionally female role challenges some previously held assumptions on single-parent families.

The growth in the rate of single fatherhood has not garnered much public attention. Some people feel these fathers have yet to receive the recognition they deserve. In an article in the *Christian Science Monitor*, Shira J. Boss writes: "Rather than being celebrated today, single fathers remain largely invisible. They almost never see themselves portrayed in popular culture, either as single parents or responsible men. When fathers do get attention, it is often negative." Boss argues that single fathers are often stigmatized as not possessing the nurturing qualities that society assumes is innate in mothers. British journalist Gavin Evan concurs, arguing in the *New Statesman* that the role played by single fathers in Great Britain is not respected. "[Single fathers] are often viewed—and view ourselves—as interlopers in someone else's world."

While these writers are among those who maintain that single fathers face bias, statistics indicate that those single-parent families are more likely to be financially secure than single-mother households are. A key argument against mother-only families has been that they are the most likely to be impoverished; this poverty is considered by many analysts to lead to an increase in violence, teenage pregnancy, and drug use among children in these households. According to 1995 Census Bureau statistics, 58 percent of mother-only families live, at best, a little above the poverty line. In contrast, only 33 percent of single-father families live under such circumstances.

The role of men in families, as well as throughout society, has changed throughout the years. In the following chapter, the authors consider whether men's roles have improved.

> "All men need do to protect and
> promote their privilege is to coast
> along with the patriarchal status
> quo."

SOCIETY FAVORS MEN

Allan G. Johnson

In the following viewpoint, Allan G. Johnson argues that society is patriarchal and that male privilege is taken for granted. According to Johnson, the presence of this male privilege means that women and minorities are viewed as outsiders and certain issues, such as violence by men against women and the part men play in gender oppression, are consequently ignored. Johnson is a sociologist and a teacher at Hartford College for Women in Connecticut.

As you read, consider the following questions:

1. According to Johnson, when are women made invisible in society?
2. In the author's view, how does male invisibility place responsibility and blame on the victim of gender oppression?
3. When is the only time men are described as special interest groups, according to the author?

Adapted and reprinted from the chapter entitled, "What Patriarchy?" in *The Gender Knot: Unraveling Our Patriarchal Legacy*, by Allan G. Johnson, by permission of Temple University Press. ©1997 by Allan G. Johnson. All rights reserved.

Perhaps the most efficient way to keep patriarchy going is to promote the idea that it doesn't exist in the first place. Patriarchy, we might say, is a just a figment of angry feminist imagination. Or, if it does exist, it's by reputation only, a shadow of its former self that no longer amounts to much in men's and women's lives. To pull this off, you have to be willing to engage in a lot of denial, but you can also use some key supporting arguments: that patriarchy doesn't exist because many women seem better off than many men; that the generally miserable lot of the modern man contradicts the idea of male privilege; that women and men are each affected by parallel versions of a common oppression; and that men and women are equal co-creators of every aspect of social life, including patriarchy and gender inequality. This mind-numbing mixture serves patriarchy well by leading us in every direction but the one that counts—toward a clear understanding of what's really going on.

THE BENEFITS OF MALE INVISIBILITY

A major way to maintain male privilege is to devalue women by making them and what they do invisible. This happens, for example, when cleaning the house or taking care of children is viewed as "nonwork," or when a woman's ideas are ignored, only to be noticed and adopted when suggested by a man. But social life is full of paradox: men are also made invisible in important ways, but invisibility, rather than working against their interests, usually works for them.

One way that this works is through the male-identified character of patriarchy itself. Because patriarchal culture designates men and masculinity as reference points for people in general, maleness is the taken-for-granted backdrop—the sea in which we swim. This makes it the last thing that stands out as remarkable. When we refer to humanity as "man," for example, maleness blends into humanness, and men can enjoy the comfort and security of not being marked as other or outsider. In contrast, "female" stands out as a marked category of outsiders in relation not simply to men, but to humanity in general. If "everyman" is everyone, then woman is something else and therefore problematic, something that needs to be figured out. The same kind of invisibility occurs around race: we hardly ever call attention to the race of whites in the news, for example, because in a white-dominated society, whiteness is the standard—the assumed race. Only deviations from the dominant group are marked for special attention. So it is routine to mark women and blacks and other minorities as exceptions (policewoman, black physician,

Native American artist, Asian American executive, and so on), a practice that underscores the normative and therefore taken-for-granted standing of men and whites. What is ironic in such cases is that male gender and white race so dominate social life that they become, in a sense, socially invisible. Unlike the invisibility of women and racial and ethnic minorities, this supports privilege by allowing men and whites to move through the world with relatively little awareness of the causes or consequences of *male* privilege and *white* privilege and the social oppression they involve.

In general, women are made invisible when they do something that might elevate their status, such as raising children into healthy adults or coming up with a brilliant idea in a business meeting. Men, however, are often made invisible when their behavior is socially undesirable and might raise questions about the appropriateness of male privilege. Although the vast majority of violent acts are perpetrated by men, for example, news accounts rarely call attention to the gender of those who rape, kill, beat, and torture others, while characteristics such as race, ethnicity, and age are routinely highlighted as socially significant. Instead, we read about mobs, crowds, people, students, gangs, citizens, youths, fans, workers, militants, party members, teenagers, armies, and so on—ungendered categories of people that presumably are as likely to include women as men. If a crowd of women gathered to make a newsworthy event, however, one can be sure they would be identified as women, not merely as a crowd; but such attention is rarely paid to maleness per se. And on those rare occasions when someone mentions statistics on male violence and suggests this might be a problem worth looking at, the response is yawning impatience ("Oh, this again?") or, more likely, a torrent of objections to the male-bashing straw man defense: "You're accusing *all* men of being murderers and rapists!"

MEN'S VIOLENCE IS IGNORED

When the media do identify male gender, they rarely make much of it, even when an event or issue is clearly related to gender. When a gang of black males brutally raped and beat a white woman in New York's Central Park in 1989, for example, everyone had an opinion about the significance of race in what happened. But hardly anyone seemed interested in the fact that *men* had brutally victimized a *woman*, an event that occurs in the United States at epidemic rates. With numbing regularity, we hear reports of violent crimes perpetrated by men, from wife beating, stalking, and murder to the gunning down of workers and bystanders by disgruntled employees to mass murder as an instrument of national policy. Yet rarely do we hear the simple statement that the perpetrators of such acts are almost always men. Nor do we take seriously the idea that men's pervasive involvement in such violence provides a clue to understanding what's happening and why. No one suggests, for example, that an ethic of male dominance might be connected to the use of violence or that there is good reason to limit the male population's opportunities to harm others. Note, however, the radically different response when members of minorities are the focus. The fact that most early AIDS victims were gay men, for example, brought demands to quarantine and repress the entire gay population, even though most gay men didn't have AIDS. Teenage *pregnancy*—a state that describes women, not men—is a hot topic in the United States, but not male *insemination* of teenage girls. And if people of color did violence to whites at the rate that the male population produces violence against women, there would be national mobilization to do something to contain this "dangerous population."

Selective male invisibility shapes how we perceive and think about gender issues. Gender oppression, for example, is routinely discussed as a *women's* issue rather than as a men's issue, making male gender invisible as part of the problem. Women become a "special interest group" when they work against gender oppression, whereas men are never seen as a special interest group when they do *not* and passively or actively benefit from it. Whether it's job discrimination, sexual harassment, or violence, gender issues typically are seen as problems for women—the category of people who are victimized. Gender issues are rarely seen as problems for men, the category of people who actually do the victimizing and whose privilege is rooted in the same system that promotes women's oppression. Job discrimination, the glass ceiling, and the double bind that plagues working mothers are all defined as women's issues even though men are the primary beneficiaries, the ones who make most of it happen, and the ones in the best position to do something about it.

If male gender is invisible, then patriarchy also is invisible, and we go around acting as though men have nothing to do with something that is, by definition, organized around gender. In the simplest sense this is illogical, because something can't be about gender and yet only be about women. If something happens to women simply because they are women, then we also have to understand why it *doesn't* happen to men simply because they happen to be men. But male invisibility is more than illogical, for it also loads both responsibility and blame onto the victim by implying that oppression is an issue for those who suffer from it but not for those who benefit from or perpetrate it. It's like defining racism as a "black problem" or toxic waste as an issue only for those who breathe, eat, or drink it and not for those who produce it or profit from it.

MEN IGNORE OPPRESSION

Defining oppression as a problem only for the oppressed is as old as oppression itself. It doesn't protect or enhance the status of men, whites, and the wealthy to look critically at systems that privilege them over women, racial minorities, and the working and lower classes. Instead, the path of least resistance is to be charitable or to focus on how oppressed groups can solve "their" problems, resolve "their" issues, or advance "their" standing as having "special interests." But advantaged, dominant groups are rarely portrayed as problematic or even as groups. Whites and men are almost never described as special interest groups except for occasional references to radical fringe groups such as the Ku Klux Klan, the Aryan Nation, or skinheads, who are never mistaken for whites as a whole. Dominant groups avoid scrutiny because their position enables them to define their own interests as those of society as a whole. Mainstream elements of racism and sexism daily promote the interests of whites and men. All men need do to protect and promote their privilege is to coast along with the patriarchal status quo—mentoring and promoting people who look like them, avoiding domestic work, and passing laws and setting policies that reflect a male-centered, male-identified, male-dominated world. Nothing much is made of it; no "special interests" at work here. But those who struggle against the consequences of patriarchy are another story. They are the "other," the outsiders trying to get in, the seekers after affirmative action and other "special" considerations that would advance them at the expense of others.

If oppression is visible only as an issue for oppressed groups, then privileged groups don't have to feel responsible or accountable or even involved. Men can feel good, even virtuous, when they show any concern for "women's issues" or just don't behave in overtly sexist ways. They can regard the slightest gesture in support of gender equality or fairness—from saying they favor equal pay to doing the dinner dishes—as a sign of what good people they are. And men can take comfort from the illusion that women can achieve justice for themselves by resolving *women's* issues with some help from benevolent men but without radically affecting men's lives or privilege or how patriarchal society is organized, including its male-identified core values.

Many men will object to the very idea that male privilege exists, but their objection also insists on a kind of invisibility that patriarchy depends on. Few men realize how much their lives would change if women weren't treated as a minority (just as whites don't see how they benefit from the oppression of racial minorities). Instead, men take credit for their hard work and achievements without taking into account how much harder it would have been if they had had to compete with women on a level playing field or do without the supportive (and unpaid) domestic labor that so many wives and mothers perform. Because patriarchy defines women as subordinate and "other," men can take women's exclusion from serious competition for granted. As a result, men have been rudely awakened by women's entry into hitherto male-only workplaces. When men complain about the advantage some women gain from affirmative action, they ignore centuries of pro-male affirmative action that, in spite of the women's movement, continues as the largely unexceptional default condition under patriarchy.

The social invisibility of male gender perpetuates patriarchy, just as the invisibility of whiteness as a race perpetuates racism. The more invisible male gender is, the more gender problems like violence and discrimination are identified with women and the less likely we are to notice that patriarchy even exists as an oppressive system.

"Males have achieved the greatest accomplishments of civilization, yet are widely perceived to be brutal, villainous or incompetent."

SOCIETY IS BIASED AGAINST MEN

R.F. Doyle

In the following viewpoint, R.F. Doyle asserts that men are denigrated and discriminated against by society. He contends that the government, feminists, the media, and others have fostered this bias by championing the causes of women through anti-male laws and unbalanced reporting on men's and women's issues. As a result, Doyle argues, men have been disparaged and unfairly characterized as oppressors. Doyle is the founder and president of the Men's Defense Association, an organization that seeks to improve the rights of men, particularly in the divorce courts. He is also the editor-in-chief of the *Liberator*, the magazine of the Men's Defense Association.

As you read, consider the following questions:

1. According to Doyle, how have social workers exacerbated anti-male bias?
2. Why does the author consider feminism irrational?
3. Why is the "men's movement" more a concern than female misandry, in Doyle's view?

Excerpted from R.F. Doyle, *The Men's Manifesto: A Commonsense Approach to Gender Issues* (Forest Lake, MN: Poor Richard's Press, 1995). Reprinted with permission from the publisher.

Esther Vilar, in her best seller, *The Manipulated Man*, calls the American male "the most exploited, the most suppressed, the most manipulated man on the face of the earth." Dual discrimination—pro-female (a perversion of chivalry) and anti-male ("misandry," meaning hatred of men, manhood and fatherhood)—is everywhere. This double standard exists in many fields—domestic relations, employment, crime punishment, and in our very image.

Women Do Not Face Discrimination

This bias is so institutionalized, it is taken for granted. The commonly accepted notion, the basic premise of women's lib, has long been that discrimination against women is greater than that against men. This is more than fashionable nonsense; it is a bizarre hoax. As many people cannot distinguish ladies from women, many also cannot distinguish truth from falsehood or right from wrong. This is explained by a founder of modern psychology, William James, who noted that, "There is nothing so absurd that, if it is repeated often enough, it will not become accepted."

In modern times there are few expectations of women and many expectations of men. Indeed, a good case can be made that western women are the most pampered creatures on earth, like sacred cows.

Political correctness is the big trend among social levelers today. Children's rights, as we know, are widely revered. Everyone knows the support women receive, but men? Nothing. The very term, "men's rights," reeks of political incorrectness. It turns off conventional liberals and conservatives alike. This enormous reservoir of sentiment makes judicial and social reform incredibly difficult.

Blurring Gender Distinctions

A large segment of the population seems to be at war with normal life. Some have mounted an ill-conceived move to rid us of all distinctions between men and women, to move toward an androgynous society. They denounce masculinity as "macho," and likewise denigrate true femininity. Rambo and John Wayne are bogeymen, except it's OK for women to imitate them; witness the many actresses clumsily playing tough cops and other male roles. This phenomenon is too widespread to be attributed to a mix-up in hormones. Its adherents seem to consider sexual characteristics restrictive and to resent traditionally distinct members of either gender. It tends to erode the biological polarity between the sexes, which is so essential to life itself. Indeed past civilizations that lost these distinctions have ceased to exist.

When it suits their purposes, "feminists" consider the sexes both identical, e.g., in employment, and different, e.g., in child custody—a classic "have their cake and eat it too" situation. They would mandate social integration and the "right" for women to elbow their way into men's schools and clubs (but not vice versa, of course). Thus, to promote less important rights, freedom of association is trampled on.

MEN ARE DENIGRATED

Males have achieved the greatest accomplishments of civilization, yet are widely perceived to be brutal, villainous or incompetent. Ads denigrating men are common in the media. Meanwhile, women are practically canonized by simple virtue of being female. One Pennsylvania legislator declared on the floor of the state senate that "A woman is born clean and decent. If she is bad it is because a man made her that way." Female glorification is further demonstrated by the, seriously taken, demand for a statue of a "combat woman" to be erected at the Vietnam War Memorial to specially and separately memorialize the eight women who died in Vietnam, contrasted with 58,000 men who died there. Sexual assault propaganda . . . demonstrates regnant anti-male hysteria.

Consider the "women and children first" slogan. Consider the horror with which killing or maiming women and children is looked upon, as opposed to killing or maiming men. Actually, chivalry is not bothersome, if restricted to ladies, and if gentlemen likewise receive their due.

The attack on males and manhood may be a rebellion against authority, with which men are often identified, or were. Ironically these sentiments adversely affect women also, because attacks on manhood are attacks on all humanity. . . .

THE CAUSES OF ANTI-MALE HATRED

Anti-male prejudice is a square dance of officials and assorted other fools. What motivates them? Reasons include a massive perversion of chivalry, fad, self-aggrandizement, and Freud's discovery—penis envy.

Neither liberals nor conservatives have been friends of the male sex, but there is a difference. Many liberals are seminally opposed to that essence of manhood, rugged individualism, as well as to such other things as property rights. Adolescent egalitarians listing to port hold the notion that all persons are equally

deserving of earthly goods, that justice and peace on earth demands equal distribution of wealth regardless of effort ("to each
according to his needs"). They favor big government, with all the
mischief that entails. Conservatives generally uphold commonsense principles, but are too naïve to grasp that misandry is antithetical to these principles.

WOMEN ARE THE ELITE

There is a good social reason why men as a class should be worried. The disadvantaged minority (women) has become the ruling elite. While it's all very well to be altruistic towards women
and to support equality, the fact is laws now give women first
preference in society. Women are taking our jobs, our promo-
tions, and our educational opportunities. They now have the right
to dissolve our marriage without our consent, take all our posses-
sions, and take our children with them. The matriarchy places restrictions on the use of language, courting practices and the right
to take men to the cleaners in the courts for sexual harassment.

Alan Barron, *Liberator*, December 1997.

In his *A History of Marriage and Family*, Australian Professor Willy-
stine Goodsell posits that the causes of modern Western social
decline are identical to those which caused the fall of the Ro-
man Empire. Women took on nontraditional roles when men
left to fight the Punic Wars, and remained in those roles after the
wars. This led to promiscuity, divorce and widespread demoralization. One need not be a college professor to see the parallels.

The former appoint themselves protectors of frail womanhood (The Galahad Complex). Unless they have led a very shel-
tered life, many of their actions and pontifications about gender
issues are naïve and stupid, sometimes downright criminally so.
As Dickens said, "The law is an ass, an idiot."

The latter will enact any abomination a fad-conscious public
desires—for votes. Fear of the powerful women's lib jugger-
naught influences their thinking. P.J. O'Rourke aptly calls them *A
Parliament of Whores*.

GOVERNMENT AND LEGAL BIASES

Big Brother is increasingly intruding into our lives. The primary
concerns of any bureaucracy are to justify its existence and expand its operation. Bureaucrats aspire to replace "the man in the
family," control the lives of the thusly-created dependents and
assume responsibility for their needs. Witness:

• Judges, police, and social "workers" are taking over the role of fathers.

• Social "workers" encourage wives to kick husbands out and eagerly provide courts with supporting rationale for awarding maternal custody, to build case loads and ultimately their empire. They lobby for ever harsher anti-male legislation, which only creates more need for themselves. They oppose realistic reforms (such as tightening eligibility and father custody), because their careers depend on existence of the support problem.

• Another entire bureaucracy has grown up around the collection of alimony, palimony, and support. Local governments have turned into giant collection agencies for divorcees; it is one of their largest functions.

George Orwell, call your office.

Why do bureaucrats fear and sabotage a society of morally and financially healthy families? Because they have so much to lose from it.

Lawyers share with wives the legalized plunder of divorce; it's one of their biggest sources of income. Voluntary reform will not spring from this quarter.

Feminism Is a Hoax

"Feminists" wallow in rhetoric about female victimization. Besides preaching misandry, the basic premise of women's lib is that women are more discriminated against than men. That is the biggest hoax in the Western world.

Feminism has become a veritable religion. Government and philanthropists throw vast sums of money at its crockpot of programs, philosophies and jamborees. Every state has generously funded a network of commissions on the status of women, despite the fact that women, in general, are financially as well off as men. Battered women's shelters are also funded, despite the absence of justification. These establishments serve as headquarters for covens of feminoids primarily to pursue their own agendas and only secondarily to help these alleged victims.

Feminism is irrational and socially destructive. Consider: Spokeswomen profess to seek equality but demand special privilege. They demand the advantages men have earned without the disadvantages, like having to earn them. They demand equal representation in the boardrooms of industry, but not in the grubby jobs or among the burned-out inhabitants of skid row. That's like wanting a one-sided coin.

Equal rights imply equal responsibility. The more responsibilities women reject, the more unequal they make themselves.

Understanding Women's Lib

This outfit begrudges veterans benefits, conveniently ignoring the sacrifices of veterans, including the thousands of acres of graves of men killed defending the very existence of this country. Their wild demands would not be possible without these sacrifices. That is called biting the hand. . . . They consider women too fragile to be pinched in an office, but tough enough to engage in combat! [Author and civil rights expert] Dr. Thomas Sowell put it best when he said, "In reality, the crusade for civil rights ended years ago. The scramble for special privilege, for turf, and for image is what continues today under that banner and with that rhetoric. . . ."

Women's lib is a "ladies'" auxiliary of the radical left. The hard core embraces Marxism, although Gloria Steinem will admit only to being socialist. Prime purposes of feminism are to establish a lesbian-socialist republic and to dismantle the family unit.

Women's lib is no joke. Neither should these hydrophobic harridans be taken too seriously. Even including their camp followers, these modern sophists are only a vociferous minority presumptuously claiming to represent the views and interests of all women. Sane women invariably eschew them.

The struggle for men's rights is positive, not a reaction to women's lib. It is inevitable that the two philosophies clash—and they do—head on.

Riddle: Is feminism a cure for which there is no disease, or a disease for which there is no cure?

The Media Ignores Men

An important reason the public is little aware of men's issues is that the media, electronic and printed, serves the lowest common intellectual denominator, tending toward the sensational and the nonsensical. Together with libraries and bookstores, the media is awash with feminism which it promotes and parrots as if prophetic, functioning practically as its bulletin board. Media worshippers enumerate, analyze, deplore and sulk about their complaints. Entire forests have given their lives for this purpose.

Men's more legitimate gripes and philosophies are censored as if heresy, although balance is feigned by publication of writings from anti-male male authors, under the guise of "masculinist" material.

Several big name entertainers, long on talent, but short on intellect, have clambered aboard the feminist bandwagon. Actors Ed Asner and Alan Alda come to mind.

Greed is a primary cause of divorce. The assurance of winning all motivates women to initiate at least eighty percent of divorces, confident that somewhere out there (many know precisely with whom) lies a better life. Most women would not divorce without these incentives.

Divorced and unmarried mothers are the largest group of welfare recipients, some because they have no pride or enjoy ripping off the public, others because they need a safety net when dismissed ex-husbands cannot or will not pay their freight. Whatever the motivation, most are parasitic.

As *Liberator* writer, Muldoon X says, AFDC [Aid to Families with Dependent Children] seems to be a heaven for bums and brood sows.

A False Men's Movement

Can victims be blamed for their plight? Damn right they can! Men themselves let it happen. We meekly accepted false accusations. We rolled over like submissive dogs before anti-male hysteria. Like helpless animals caught in car headlights, we stood by while our rights and responsibilities were taken away. We abdicated our trousers.

In the last decade, a "men's movement" has come into existence, made up of disillusioned feminists, masochists, homosexuals and other lost souls seeking salvation in male bonding, drumming, mythopoetry, etc. They meet at "warrior weekends," where they beat drums, denounce masculinity, cry a lot, and grope at each other in "consciousness raising" sessions, presided over by charlatans selling paraphernalia, conducting seminars, giving "massages," or reading poetry. Many are sex melders convinced there is something wrong (macho) with the traditional male image. Presumptuously claiming to represent men's liberation, this outfit would like to liberate us all right, from our manhood!

Female misandrists are overt and honest about it. We, at the Men's Defense Association (MDA), grudgingly respect that. It is easily defended against. We are more concerned with *covert* misandry, attacks from the rear by nominal males masquerading as part of the men's movement, or even as *the* men's movement.

Male characteristics are also liabilities; the qualities that cause us to excel—ego, rugged individualism—prevent us from cooperating in our defense. . . .

Overcoming Discrimination

Martin Luther King took the bows for overthrowing racial discrimination, but it was probably Malcolm X who scared Whites into it. The MDA hopes the culprits responsible for the present unacceptable situation will clean up their own houses, so that this burden does not devolve upon victims. But if it does, so be it. We will no longer counsel self-restraint. Officials beware, there are many justifiably angry divorced men out here, enough to make Shay's Rebellion look like a picnic. You would be well advised to restore justice. As JFK said, "Those who prevent peaceful revolution necessitate violent revolution." These words are harsh, but how else can one adequately address harsh realities?

The ideal solution is for legitimate, heterosexual male victims to band together and non-violently overcome discrimination! Cooperation has often been attempted, but the efforts have always self-destructed. Money is one of many problems. With a fraction of the resources available to women's lib or of the cost of incarcerating adult criminals sprung from fatherless delinquents, we could mount a strong counter force for gender justice and for a civilized world.

Beneath the corruption, our political institutions are creations of wise and prudent men, and repositories of much that is good. It is these very institutions that make our society function, however imperfectly. Contrary to Marx, we should build a superior social order upon the basic structure, rather than the ruins, of the old. The Men's Defense Association is willing to try.

| "We must recover a sense of what it means to be manly."

MASCULINITY NEEDS TO BE RESTORED

Waller R. Newell

In the following viewpoint, Waller R. Newell maintains that young men need to learn a positive version of masculinity that encourages honor, pride, and respect for women. He asserts that masculinity has been distorted since the 1960s, leading to misogyny and violence toward women. Newell contends that society needs to channel certain boyish traits, such as a desire to be heroic, in positive directions and teach these boys how to become honorable men. Newell is a professor of political science and philosophy at Carleton University in Ottawa, Canada.

As you read, consider the following questions:

1. What has been the result of the baby-boomer belief that children do not need masculine role models, in Newell's view?
2. According to Newell, what are some ways in which men and women are different?
3. In the author's opinion, why do young men get body piercings?

Excerpted from Waller R. Newell, "The Crisis of Manliness," *The Weekly Standard*, August 3, 1998. Reprinted with the permission of the publisher. Copyright 1998, News America Inc.

The last 30 years have witnessed a prolonged effort at social engineering throughout our public and educational institutions. Its purpose is to eradicate any psychological and emotional differences between men and women, on the grounds that any concept of manliness inevitably leads to arrogance and violence towards women and to rigid hierarchies that exclude the marginalized and powerless. This experiment was meant to reduce violence and tensions between the sexes. And yet, during this same period, "macho" violence and stress between men and women may well have increased. Crime statistics suggest as much in the United States, Canada, and the United Kingdom— the countries where the feminist social experiment stigmatizing manliness has had the greatest latitude to prove itself.

NO ROLE MODELS

As the book [The Divorce Culture] by Barbara Dafoe Whitehead confirmed, absent fathers are one of the strongest predictors of violence among young men in the United States, at least as important as poverty, lack of education, or minority status. The ease with which men of my baby-boomer generation have abdicated our roles as fathers is undoubtedly connected with feminism and the sexual revolution of the 1960s. Boomers were told that we shouldn't be hung up about providing masculine role models for children and should do whatever made us happiest, including escape an unsatisfying marriage. After all, to hold things together for the sake of the children would restrict both men and women to old-fashioned "patriarchal" responsibilities. The results of this hard, bright credo of selfishness are today's underfathered young men, many of them from broken homes, prone to identify their maleness with aggression because they have no better model to go by.

This generation's experience is summed up in a brilliant, pathetic scene from Atom Egoyan's film Family Viewing. The central character, a teenaged boy, drifts in and out of his divorced father's house. The father is totally preoccupied with his relationship with a younger woman. The boy's only solid human contact is with his dying grandmother, shunted to a nursing home lest she spoil the father's swinging lifestyle. One day the boy digs out some family videos. At first, he sees a backyard barbecue with happy children and his parents when they were still together. Suddenly, the film jumps to the father and his new girlfriend having sex. The father simply taped over the family movies, literally erasing his son's connection with the only secure part of his childhood.

It seems plain enough that we are missing the boat about manliness, for there are forms of pride and honor that would be good to impart to young males. Indeed, manly honor, and shame at failing to live up to it, are the surest means of promoting respect for women. Equally, manly anger and combativeness can provide energy for a just cause. Horrified as we are by the cult of warrior violence in the Balkans or Rwanda, we may have gone too far toward the opposite extreme in the Western democracies. As journalist Michael Kelly observed, "There are fewer and fewer people, and they are older and older people, who accept what every 12-year-old in Bihac knows: that there are some things worth dying and killing for." Abolitionism in the ante-bellum United States, the Allies' defeat of Nazi Germany, and the civil-rights movement of the '60s would never have succeeded without the legitimate expression of anger against injustice. The point is not to eradicate honor and pride from the male character, but to re-channel those energies . . . to some constructive moral purpose.

MASCULINITY IS CONSIDERED ARCHAIC

The very notion that being male involves some version of masculine behavior—strength, courtesy, courage, chivalry, virility, restraint—seems nearly as archaic as "manliness" itself. Does anyone use the word anymore, except in the sense of a caricature? Do fathers still urge their boys to be men? For as surely as males are freed from the confines of manly behavior, they may loosen the bonds of civilized conduct.

Philip Terzian, *Women's Quarterly*, Autumn 1996.

To do this, we must recover a sense of what it means to be manly—honorable, brave, self-restrained, zealous in behalf of a good cause, with feelings of delicacy and respect toward loved ones. For if young men are cut off from this positive tradition of manly pride, their manliness will reemerge in crude and retrograde forms. Some 30 years ago, the Rolling Stones recorded a misogynist rant called "Under My Thumb." Today, it is one of the songs that fans most frequently request of these aging shamans of adolescent attitudinizing. In three decades, tension between men and women not only has not disappeared but may actually have intensified, and we must wonder whether the experiment in social engineering itself is one reason why.

For hostility towards women is an aberration of male behavior. If, as the prevailing orthodoxy contends, the male gender were intrinsically aggressive, hegemonic, and intolerant, then by definition male behavior could never improve. The message young males receive from feminist reasoning is not, You should be ashamed of liking "Under My Thumb," but, That's the way your gender thinks about women.

So the first step toward a sensible debate about manly pride is to rescue the positive tradition of manliness from three decades of stereotyping that conflates masculinity with violence, hegemony, and aggression. We have to recognize that men and women are moral equals, that decent and worthy men have always known this, and that, while men and women share the most important human virtues, vices, and aptitudes, they also have psychological traits that incline them toward some different activities.

MEN AND WOMEN HAVE DIFFERENT INTERESTS

According to the regnant orthodoxy, men and women should have exactly the same kinds of capacities and ambitions. They should be equally interested in becoming tycoons, winning battles, driving tractors, and nurturing children. But this is not reality. In general, men don't want to work in day-care centers or teach kindergarten, and women don't want to be truck drivers or join the military. Moreover, women are far more likely than men to leave successful jobs to devote time to families, and women under 30 are more eager for lasting marriages and numerous children than women of their parents' generation (doubtless yearning for what their parents denied them). We should recognize at last that, as long as women are guaranteed an equal opportunity to pursue whatever occupation they want, it does not matter that men and women on the whole still choose different vocations. Remaining injustices should be addressed by procedural liberalism, which has always brought the most solid progress. We should stop trying to reengineer the human soul to prevent boys from being boyish, while encouraging all forms of self-expression in girls.

All that 30 years of behavioral conditioning has done is drive maleness underground and distort it by severing it from traditional sources of masculine restraint and civility. The gurus of sensitivity have tried to convince men to become open, fluid, nonhegemonic, and genderless beings who are unafraid to cry. But little boys still want to play war and shoot up the living room with plastic howitzers, and we can't give them all Ritalin. Psychologists have begun to express concern about our educational institutions' readiness to pathologize what once would have been regarded as boyish high spirits—rough-housing, "hating" girls, locker-room language—and to treat ordinary immaturity with powerful drugs.

Again, the point is to channel these energies into the development of character. Boys and young men still want to be heroes, and the way to educate them to treat girls and women with respect is to appeal to their heroism, not to try to blot it out. Look at those kids performing daring flips on their skateboards, or sailing on their Rollerblades into the heaviest downtown traffic like warriors contemptuous of danger. They are almost always males. Look at that squeegee kid with his shaved head and horsehair plume, decked out like some road-warrior Achilles. Walk into one of those high-voltage computer emporiums, selling our century's most potent icon for the extension of human mastery over the cosmos. Who are the salesmen? Almost always cocky young men, celebrities-in-waiting in dark suits and moussed hair, hooked on the sheer power of it all.

INFANTILE MALES

Channel surf on your television late at night and sample the rock videos. Nearly all the bands in those rock videos are male, snarling or plaintive over the world's confusions and their erotic frustrations, oozing belligerence alternating with Byronic alienation and a puppyish longing for attention. Their names (Goo Goo Dolls) and attitudes (the lead singer of Radiohead is wheeled around a supermarket in a giant shopping cart curled up like an overgrown 5-year-old) combine an infantile longing to return to childhood with in-your-face suspicion and distrust.

And what else would one expect, since so many of the families into which they were born ended in divorce? By denying and repressing their natural inclination to manliness, we run the risk of abandoning them to such infantile posturing. When they pierce their bodies, it is because they want to experience moral and erotic constraint. Having failed to find an authority they can respect, someone to guide them from boyish impetuosity to a mature and manly vigor of judgment, they confuse authority with oppression. Still, cast adrift in a world without any limitations, they want there to be a price to pay for their hedonism. Since no one will lead them back to the great ethical and religious traditions that set these limits on the highest intellectual and spiritual level, they pierce their bodies in a crude simulacrum of traditional restraint. And, in that, they reveal not only the wondrous capacity of spirited young people to see through the aridity of the governing orthodoxies but also the potential for an ennobling transformation.

Virtue Should Be Fostered

It is precisely in a traditional understanding of manly pride and honor that we will find the only sure basis for respect between men and women. The best way of convincing young men to treat women with respect is to educate them in the traditional virtues, which make it a disgrace to treat anyone basely, dishonestly, or exploitatively. Moreover, the surest way of raising young men to treat young women as friends rather than as objects for sexual exploitation is to appeal to their natural longing to be honored and esteemed by the young women to whom they are attracted. When our erotic attraction to another is properly directed, it leads us to cultivate the virtues of moderation, honesty, gratitude, and compassion that make us worthy of love in the eyes of the beloved. We try to be virtuous because we want to be worthy of being loved.

One thing is sure: Given our current confusion over the meaning of manliness, we have nothing to lose by re-opening the issue.

| "Much of our culture is built upon a tolerance, even a reverence, for an aggressive . . . version of manhood."

MASCULINITY IS DANGEROUS

Susan Douglas

Masculinity emphasizes aggressiveness and leads to violence, argues Susan Douglas in the following viewpoint. Douglas, a professor of communications studies at the University of Michigan, states that if aggressive behavior is tolerated as part of maleness, then the result will be greater violence toward others, particularly women. Society should not foster or accept aggressiveness as part of masculine behavior, she contends; instead, young men should be encouraged to recognize peaceableness and respect as part of masculinity.

As you read, consider the following questions:

1. According to FBI statistics, as cited by the author, how much more often are athletes reported to the police for sexual assault than the average male college student?
2. In Douglas's view, what is the dominant image of masculinity?
3. According to Bernard Lefkowitz, as quoted by Douglas, what do schools not consider to be a serious issue?

Reprinted from Susan Douglas, "The Making of a Bully," *The Progressive*, October 1997, by permission of *The Progressive*, 409 E. Main St., Madison, WI 53703.

The man was screaming at a teenage boy. "Why are you being so nice to him?" he yelled. "*Why?*"

The boy looked sheepish, and was silent.

"You hit him, and you hit him *hard* next time," the older man
insisted.

CONFLICTING MESSAGES

I was out walking the dog on a trail that surrounds the local
high school, and I had stumbled upon football practice—block-
ing practice, to be precise. I didn't know this at first. I heard
only the man's voice, serrated and alien, cutting through the
sounds of crickets and rustling leaves and disrupting my rich in-
ner thoughts about what to make for dinner and where to get
my daughter's school supplies.

She and I had just reviewed "Promoting Responsible Behavior,"
a flier sent home with her on the first day of school that listed
"guidelines for a respectful, self-disciplined, and caring school
community." Hitting, pushing, and any other forms of physical
aggression are *verboten*, and now children as young as six can be
overheard talking about respecting others' "personal space."

The young man berated for being a wuss was probably
drilled in the school district's "conflict-management curriculum," also touted in the flier. What was he to do? Should he
learn to hit as hard as possible? Or would he be nice and fail?
How would he manage to be peaceable yet a brute?

VIOLENT MALES

The coach's instructions caught me at the height of a police scan-
dal in New York. White male officers holding positions of enormous power and authority conducted a sexually monstrous invasion of a black man's body. At the time, I was also reading Our
Guys by Bernard Lefkowitz, his disturbing account of the 1989
rape of a retarded girl in Glen Ridge, New Jersey. The stars of the
school's football team attacked her with a baseball bat and broom
handle, no less. Like the cops in New York, these guys assumed
they'd never get caught, or that such things would be tolerated.

The cops were "rogues," "renegades," according to New
York officials. But Lefkowitz's account is much more chilling. It
was the revered jock culture of Glen Ridge—one that reigns
supreme in high schools throughout the land—that produced
and then sought to dismiss the despicable acts against the girl
in the basement.

Feminists get into trouble when we suggest that there might
be a deep and pathological crisis surrounding masculinity in

this country. We get into even bigger trouble when we ask about the relationship between cherished male institutions—football teams, military academies, police squads, frat houses—and brutal, criminal behavior. We are male-bashers, or we are making glib causal associations, ignoring the good these institutions do. No matter that as macho an institution as the FBI documented, in the mid-1980s, that athletes in sports in which aggressiveness and physical force are prided—most notably football and basketball players—were reported to the police for sexual assault 38 percent more often than the average male college student.

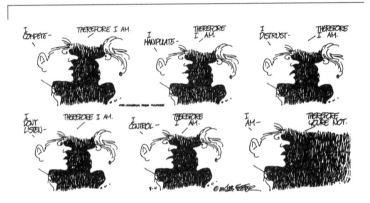

But all too many news stories—from the scandals in the military to the epidemic of police brutality and the rapes by athletes—point to the truth that much of our culture is built upon a tolerance, even a reverence, for an aggressive, above-the-law, bullying version of manhood.

MODERN CULTURE CAN HARM BOYS

Many feminists, for good reason, have emphasized the loss of self-esteem that all too many girls experience when they hit adolescence. But it is time now to start focusing on the boys as well. Too many boys are growing up in a culture that compels them to suppress their fundamental humanity. When that happens, those they have power over suffer, sometimes brutally.

Challenging the precepts of masculinity is virtually unspeakable in this country. But figuring out exactly what constitutes successful manhood is no easy matter, either—take a step off the tightrope one way and you're a nerd; step off in the other direction and you're a brute. Punching a guy repeatedly until his innards turn into polenta makes you a hero and a multimillionaire; biting the same guy on the ear makes you a barbarian.

Our male children confront deeply conflicting messages about their identities. Media images of New Age, compassionate men like the doctors on ER intermix with the strutting macho men in action films where the hero invariably wields a very, very big stick. We are expected to applaud the gun-toting, karate-chopping, quasi-vigilante movie heroes, yet to revile real-life bounty hunters who, just recently, behaved not unlike Steven Seagal on the screen. But despite these warring messages, the dominant image of ideal masculinity is of a guy who learned, in high school, how to hit hard. Is this really the mantle of manhood we want them to drape over their shoulders?

GIRLS ARE THREATENED

As the mother of a daughter, I worry about what harassments, or worse, she will confront from insecure guys who are trying to inflate their own image at her expense, trying to mimic what Lefkowitz calls "a grotesque version of manhood." In 1996, when she was in the first grade, and sitting on the swings during recess, a boy came up to her and said, "Suck my cock." Despite the conflict-management curriculum, the lesson that such comments are an outrage is not getting through.

Lefkowitz, in Our Guys, sees the culture in Glen Ridge—where "jocks ruled" and where "callous, abusive behavior toward girls" was an everyday occurrence in school—as typical. The press repeatedly described the retarded girl as someone "who had not progressed beyond the mental age of an eight-year-old." Ignored, notes Lefkowitz, was the fact that "the values of the community she grew up in had not progressed beyond those of a high-school pep rally." Across the country, schools didn't think that "the everyday treatment of girls by boys was a serious issue that merited discussion among faculty and students."

Not all football players are rapists, and not all cops are sadists. But Our Guys—a book every middle- and high-school teacher should read—reveals that we need to have a national conversation not just about race. We need to have one about masculinity, too.

| "Americans no longer hold strong and
universal convictions about the
solemn duties of men to their
children."

THE ROLE OF FATHERS AND HUSBANDS IS DISRESPECTED

Stephen Chapman

The importance of fatherhood and marriage is not respected, argues syndicated columnist Stephen Chapman in the following viewpoint. Chapman contends certain politicians and celebrities have popularized the dangerous idea that two-parent families are not necessary. In addition, Chapman asserts, many men do not value the role of fatherhood and have abandoned their responsibilities. He claims marriage must be restored because, rather than posing a threat to women and children, it reduces the likelihood of domestic violence and lowers the rates of poverty and juvenile crime.

As you read, consider the following questions:

1. According to Margarita Prentice, as quoted by Chapman, what is the origin of the wedding ring?
2. What percentage of incidents of domestic violence against women is committed by husbands, according to statistics cited by the author?
3. In Chapman's view, how do many Americans regard the fathers of the 1950s?

Reprinted from Stephen Chapman, "Without Benefit of Matrimony," *Washington Times*, February 22, 1995, by permission of Stephen Chapman and Creators Syndicate.

A group of Washington state legislators thinks American women face a grave danger: marriage. They want to change the wording on marriage licenses to inform those contemplating this hazardous step that neither spouse becomes the property of the other and that married partners have the right to live "free from violence and abuse." These facts presumably will come as a revelation to the women of Washington state.

State Sen. Margarita Prentice—who says "the origin of the wedding ring represents part of a chain binding the wife to her master"—believes the measure would help educate women about the perils of domestic violence, besides discouraging them from ill-considered unions. "I would say, simply, beware," she says.

The Truth About Domestic Violence

Ms. Prentice must be pleased to know that marriage has been on the decline in America for some decades now. Divorce has grown common, and out-of-wedlock births are climbing steadily. If marriage is the source of domestic violence, says David Blankenhorn in his book, "Fatherless America," we might expect domestic violence to also be on the decline.

Wrong. "The weakening of marriage has not made the home a safer place for women," he writes. "As more women are living apart from husbands and fathers, more women are being battered by men." One government study, widely reported in the press, found that 6 percent of all pregnant women are beaten by their husbands or boyfriends. But the authors failed to publicize that unmarried women are four times more likely to be battered than married women.

In fact, says Mr. Blankenhorn, "Marital status is the strongest predictor of abuse in this study—stronger than race, age, educational attainment, housing conditions or access to prenatal care." Only 9 percent of the incidents of domestic violence against women are committed by husbands. Sixty-five percent are committed by boyfriends and former husbands.

The truth, then, is the opposite of what Ms. Prentice and her co-sponsors suggest: Marriage does not so much expose women to abuse as protect them from it. Maybe it's unmarried women who need a warning.

Maligning Marriage

But the Washington lawmakers are not alone in their misunderstanding. Men and women alike have gotten used to the idea that marriage isn't necessarily healthy for women or their kids.

Dan Quayle criticized a TV show for the lead character's decision to have a child out of wedlock—and found Americans siding with Murphy Brown.

Actress Michelle Pfeiffer, when asked why she had decided to raise a child on her own, expressed a view that once would have been shocking but today is uncontroversial: "I don't want some guy in my life forever who's going to be driving me nuts." Most Americans now agree that single mothers can raise children as well as married couples and reject the view that children are generally better off in intact, two-parent homes.

Recovering Fatherhood

Our essential goal must be the rediscovery in modern society of the fatherhood idea. [Anthropologist Bronislaw] Malinowski called it the "principle of legitimacy." For every child, a legally and morally responsible adult male. Others have described this idea as the imperative of paternal investment, achieved through a parental alliance with the mother. A more familiar name for such activity is married fatherhood.

The essence of the fatherhood idea is simple. A father for every child. But in our society, few ideas could be more radical. Embracing the fatherhood idea would require a fundamental shift in cultural values and in parental behavior. No other change in U.S. family life could produce such dramatic improvement in child and societal well-being.

To recover the fatherhood idea, we must fashion a new cultural story of fatherhood. The moral of today's story is that fatherhood is superfluous. The moral of the new story must be that fatherhood is essential.

David Blankenhorn, *Fatherless America: Confronting Our Most Urgent Social Problem*, 1995.

In general, says Mr. Blankenhorn, "fatherhood has been devalued. Within the home, fathers have been losing authority; within the wider society, fatherhood has been losing esteem. Many influential people in today's public debate argue that, when all is said and done, fathers are simply not very important."

Americans no longer hold strong and universal convictions about the solemn duties of men to their children—or to the children's mother. The cultural pressures that once pushed men into accepting lifelong family obligations have grown weak. Far too many men have abandoned the responsibilities their own fathers and grandfathers took for granted.

As a result, our society has been able to compile mountains of human rubble proving that fathers are very important after all. Homes headed by a single mother suffer more poverty than any other kind, and boys who grow up in such households are especially prone to crime. Most of the worst social problems of our time—poverty, violence, drug abuse, welfare dependency, sexual irresponsibility—can be traced to the crumbling of the family.

Many Americans look askance at the fathers of the 1950s, who are generally viewed as distant authoritarians who did little for their families but come home for dinner at night and provide for material comfort. This feeling of superiority is odd, notes Mr. Blankenhorn, considering how many modern fathers, divorced or never married, fail to do either—or anything else.

To an extent generally unnoticed, Americans have responded to the collapse of the family by pretending, as Ms. Prentice and her colleagues do, that it's not necessarily a bad development. In fact, it has proven to be a terribly destructive development, particularly for women and children. Few social needs are more vital than rebuilding the family. The first step is recognizing the indispensability of fathers.

| "What does it tell a boy about his mother, . . . if a man has to be brought in to take charge?"

THE ROLE OF FATHERS IS OVEREMPHASIZED

Olga Silverstein and Beth Rashbaum

The importance of fathers in serving as role models for their sons is overemphasized, argue Olga Silverstein and Beth Rashbaum in the following viewpoint. The authors contend that while having a father in the home can be beneficial, it is inaccurate to claim that boys will fail to become masculinized if no male role model is present. According to Silverstein and Rashbaum, mothers are capable of teaching the qualities that their sons need to mature. Silverstein is a member of the emeritus faculty at the Ackerman Institute for Family Therapy in New York City, while Rashbaum is a freelance book editor and writer.

As you read, consider the following questions:

1. According to the authors, what is the worst thing about female-headed households?
2. In the authors' view, what are some examples of negative male role models?
3. What are the qualities that Silverstein and Rashbaum believe women can teach their sons?

In his book *A Choice of Heroes: The Changing Face of American Manhood*, Mark Gerzon writes: "Men today consume certain images of manhood even though the world from which they are derived may have disappeared.". . . It's probably *because* that world is in the process of disappearing that these hero images are consumed with such avidity, such a desperate desire to hold on to them. The remarkable success of the male action film genre, the proliferation of a veritable arsenal of weaponry in our toy stores, video arcades, and home video games, the bodybuilding mania of deskbound middle-class men—all these phenomena speak of a longing to recapture a heroic male past in an age when that kind of heroism is at best irrelevant. As one personal trainer describes the appeal of bodybuilding: "To be honest, you can consider yourself part of the warrior class without ever putting yourself in danger." Pop culture has responded to the irrelevance of traditional concepts of masculinity by reinstating them with a vengeance.

THE EXALTATION OF MALE ROLE MODELS

Pop psychology has done something rather similar in its response to the declining institution of fatherhood. In 1970 single-parent families—the single parent almost always being a mother—made up only 12.9 percent of those with children under eighteen; in 1980 the proportion grew to 21.5 percent; and in 1991 it was 28.9 percent. Now that men seem to be disappearing from the family unit in ever greater numbers, the women who are left behind to raise the children are being told that their sons are in dire need of male role models.

With men no longer being men in the old sense of the word, they have become "male role models"; no longer clear about what it is to be masculine, they "model" masculinity; confused about their identity as men, they have "male sex-role identities"; no longer functioning as fathers, they are "father figures."

"Missing Dads," "Life Without Father," "Mothers, Sons Going It Alone: Single Women Agonize Over How Their Boys Will Become Men," "Rise in Single Parenthood . . . Reshaping U.S."—this is just a sampling of newspaper headlines. Alarm bells are sounding throughout the nation over the phenomenon of the absentee father. And with good reason—though not the reasons that are usually given by either well-meaning newspaper writers and their psychologist and sociologist sources, or by "family values" preachers like Dan Quayle. The single most terrible thing about female-headed households is their poverty. "Almost half of all female-headed families with children under 18 live in poverty, and the median family income for two-parent families is three times that of female-headed families," according to an article in The New York Times. More than two-thirds of children under age six living in such households are poor.

MEN CAN BE IMPORTANT

There's no question in my mind that for most heterosexual women and their children, generally speaking, life with a man is better than it is without (provided the man isn't alcoholic, drug-addicted, violent, or abusive). The families of these absentee fathers need their paychecks, and certainly most of the women in these families long for male companionship, for love, for commitment, for practical help around the house and with the children, for someone with whom they can share both the joys and hardships of everyday life. Women and children alike want men and need men for all sorts of benefits, material and emotional, and numerous studies support the idea that children of both sexes do better, psychologically and intellectually, when there are two parents actively involved in their care.

That's not the story that comes across in the popular press, however. There we are told that the phenomenon of absentee fathers is most alarming not so much because it results in poverty and loneliness, and all the problems deriving from those forms of deprivation, but because it denies young boys the "male role models" they need. Thus we blame social ills on the individual, scapegoating the absentee father and often the single mother as well, rather than seeing both as victims of a social system that gives inadequate support to families while paying lavish lip service to "family values."

"Who was going to show my son how to walk [like a man]?" a woman agonized in one article. "Fathers protect, they provide, they initiate into adulthood, they bring the standards of the outside world to bear on their children," says the author of another (ignoring the fact that it is men who commit most of the crimes in the world, as well as in their own homes). Psychiatrist Frank Pittman, who scolds the "politically correct" for their mistaken belief "that a mother [is] able to show a male child how to be a man," tells us categorically that "in families where the father is absent, the mother faces an impossible task: she cannot raise a boy into a man. He must bond with a man as he grows up."

A NEIGHBOR'S CONCERN

How profoundly this notion of male role models has insinuated itself into our culture, to the point that just about every divorced, separated, widowed, or unmarried mother of sons is likely to be anguishing about how to get one of these for her boy! Even the fact that her son is doing just fine without one will not deter her, for any behavior that isn't downright macho may seem to her to signal a full-blown crisis in her child's gender identity. On my way to the elevator the other day a young neighbor confided that she was concerned about her eight-year-old son, and she wondered if I could recommend a therapist, preferably male. I knew the boy only slightly but couldn't imagine what she was worried about. He was a quiet, slightly reserved youngster, but self-assured and reasonably forthcoming for his age, as well as polite and appealing. Matthew and I had often exchanged pleasant greetings and chitchat in the lobby. So what was the problem?

SINGLE-PARENT FAMILIES ARE HEALTHY

Many single parents who divorced or didn't marry made the healthiest choice in creating a peaceful and stable home for their family.

Many well-researched studies document positive outcomes in single-parent families. "Single parenting develops the parent's independence and ability to handle a variety of situations." (Shaw, 1991) "Children benefit from increased levels of responsibility." (Amata, 1987) "Parental- and child-health outcomes were related to larger networks of social support and good communication within the single-parent family." (Hanson, 1986)

Loanda Cullen, *Single Parenting in the Nineties*, 1995.

"Matthew's a very good kid," she told me. "His teachers like him, he does well in school, he gets along with the other kids, but—I don't know how to say this—yesterday he came home crying because a bunch of toughs from the class ahead of his ganged up on him. They called him 'a fruit' and other things I can hardly repeat."

"What did he do?" I asked.

"He ran home."

"That seems wise," I commented. "He was one small boy against a group of bigger boys. What are you worried about?"

"He won't fight. He doesn't like rough games. He prefers being home and reading and building things."

"Well, what's wrong with that?" A question I might have not asked under different socioeconomic circumstances, where fighting might be more of a basic survival technique, but one that seemed appropriate for a young matron on the Upper East Side of Manhattan with a child in a prestigious private school.

"It's just that he might be different if he had a father. But he barely knows Sid. After we separated Sid virtually disappeared from our lives. He spends all of his time racking up hundreds of billable hours at his fancy law firm. So I keep thinking Matthew needs a male role model," she said.

NOT ALL MEN ARE GOOD ROLE MODELS

Perhaps Sid could be induced to spend more time with his son, I suggested—not because I think Matthew needs more male companionship in his life but because I see she does. "No, no," she protested, "I don't want him to have a driven, workaholic role model."

What about her father? "An alcoholic, and abusive on top of that," she replied.

Any brothers? "My brother is a playboy. He hates women and he hates kids and he probably hates himself." And so we went through the list. Ultimately, I had to ask her, as I have so many others, what she meant by a male role model. The distant, closed-off, unknowable-to-himself-as-well-as-others male? The successful, driven, workaholic male? The macho, angry, abusive male? The womanizing, promiscuous, unable-to-commit male? And so forth. Is *any* male better than none?

But this is begging the question. Despite the lack of viable "male role models" in a given individual's life, there certainly are many good men in this world, who could be held up to any young child as exemplary. The more fundamental issue is the very notion of a male role model as something that a young boy needs in his life if he is to become a man. Though this notion is simply the latest trendy psychological panacea for a host of societal ills, it's taken as gospel. . . .

WOMEN CAN BE ROLE MODELS

What does it tell a boy about his mother, and about women in general, if a man has to be brought in to take charge? And what does that tell him about how he's going to treat women later in life? Why not show him that women can nurture *and* lead, can be loving *and* competent, can be figures of authority *and* compassion? . . . These are not mutually exclusive qualities, and they are precisely the qualities that women have already had to develop for use in the outside world.

Certainly I have seen these qualities in hundreds of the women who have passed through my office over the years, many of them struggling with doubts about how to raise boys on their own. If women would bring into their homes the same qualities they've had so much practice using in the workplace, or if they would simply deploy the complete range of competencies that is involved in full-time mothering today, instead of "dumbing out" when their sons reach a certain age, they could be completely adequate role models if necessary—as it increasingly often is, however much we might wish otherwise.

PERIODICAL BIBLIOGRAPHY

The following articles have been selected to supplement the diverse views presented in this chapter. Addresses are provided for periodicals not indexed in the *Readers' Guide to Periodical Literature*, the *Alternative Press Index*, the *Social Sciences Index*, or the *Index to Legal Periodicals and Books*.

Frederick Clarkson	"Righteous Brothers," *In These Times*, August 5–18, 1996.
Patricia Cohen	"Daddy Dearest: Do You Really Matter?" *New York Times*, July 11, 1998.
Thomas B. Edsall	"The U.S. Male, Caught in a Cultural Shift," *Washington Post National Weekly Edition*, May 8–14, 1995. Available from 1150 15th St. NW, Washington, DC 20071.
Glamour	"Are White Men *Really* Oppressed?" May 1995.
Stephen Goode	"For Wade Horn, Fathers of Our Country Are Key to Its Survival," *Insight*, August 18, 1997. Available from 3600 New York Ave. NE, Washington, DC 20002.
Katherine Kersten	"Male Models," *American Enterprise*, November/December 1997.
Jeffrey M. Leving and Caryn M. Kenik	"The Father's Custody Case," *Trial*, January 1999.
Melissa Ludtke	"Sometimes, One Parent Is Better than Two," *New York Times*, August 16, 1997.
Janny Scott	"Hunk, He-Man, Mensch, Milquetoast: The Masks of Masculinity," *New York Times*, February 13, 1999.
Michael Segell	"The Second Coming of the Alpha Male," *Esquire*, October 1996.
Sue Shellenbarger	"Good News at Last in Battle of the Sexes: Men Are Helping More," *Wall Street Journal*, April 15, 1998.
Ron Stodghill II	"God of Our Fathers," *Time*, October 6, 1997.
Olivia Vlahos	"Where Have All the Fathers Gone?" *Women's Quarterly*, Autumn 1998. Available from P.O. Box 3058, Arlington, VA 22203-0058.
Trish Wilson	"Will Paternal Paranoia Triumph?" *On the Issues*, Winter 1997.

CHAPTER 4

WHAT WILL IMPROVE MALE/FEMALE RELATIONSHIPS?

CHAPTER PREFACE

Although most people enter a marriage believing it will last a lifetime, the divorce rate in the United States is 40 percent. Numerous solutions have been suggested for decreasing this rate, thereby improving this central male/female relationship. One approach is covenant marriage.

Since August 1997, couples marrying in Louisiana have had a choice: standard marriage, which permits no-fault divorce should either partner wish to dissolve the union, or covenant marriage, which allows divorce only after a two-year separation or under circumstances such as abuse, adultery, imprisonment for a felony, or abandonment. Standard marriage remains the popular choice; as of 1998, only 3 percent of newlyweds in Louisiana opted for covenant licenses, although some already-married couples have "upgraded" their vows. The only other state with a similar law as of this writing is Arizona.

Covenant marriage may not be widespread, but controversy exists nonetheless over its effects. Supporters assert that covenant marriage deepens commitment by encouraging couples to work out their problems. Amitai Etzioni, the founder and director of the Communitarian Network, an organization that seeks to preserve individual liberty by strengthening the foundations of civil society, writes: "[Should] only 'disposable' marriages be available to couples—or should there also be an option that encourages them to work harder at sustaining their marriages?" Etzioni praises the options provided in the legislation, maintaining that the Louisiana law gives "people the opportunity to be virtuous, but [does not penalize] them if they choose not to."

However, not everybody believes that covenant marriage offers a true choice. Opponents assert that standard marriage will be seen as less legitimate if covenant marriage gains popularity. Another caveat some observers have raised is that women, particularly those in abusive marriages, may find it more difficult emotionally and financially to seek a divorce. According to Terry A. O'Neill, the president of the Louisiana chapter of the National Organization for Women, "Those most harmed by covenant marriage's barriers to exit will be those who most need to be able to get out quickly and even secretly: victims of domestic violence."

Covenant marriage is only one of many solutions aimed at improving marriage. In the following chapter, the authors debate how marriage and other relationships between the sexes can be reshaped and improved.

| "For a woman to yield to a man is tantamount to treason in today's society. Yet it is what God requires of us."

MARRIAGES WILL IMPROVE IF WIVES SUBMIT TO THEIR HUSBANDS

Christine McClelland

Women should submit to their husbands because it is a holy act that will strengthen marriages, argues Christine McClelland in the following viewpoint. She cites a personal experience as an example of the trouble that can occur when a wife does not listen to her husband. According to McClelland, submission does not make a wife subservient. Instead, she contends, the Bible states that spouses are supposed to work together and submit to each other out of reverence for God. McClelland is an Oregon homemaker.

As you read, consider the following questions:
1. What was the author's initial definition of submission?
2. Why does the author believe that the woman described in Proverbs 31 is not subservient?
3. According to biblical passages, as cited by McClelland, how are men accountable to their wives?

Reprinted from Christine McClelland, "That Ugly 'S' Word," Moody, July/August 1998, with permission from the author.

"Now I don't want you to do too much today," my husband said as he gathered his lunch and coat to go out the door. "You know the doctor wants you to rest for the next six weeks." "Yes, I know, Dear. I just have one thing planned. I'm going to plant some pansies." I tried to look innocent. "And that's all?" "That's it." "Why don't I believe you?" I heard him muttering as he walked down the porch toward the car. "It's just six pansies, Dear," I called after him. "Don't worry."

The Gardening Experience

Everyone says I can take an ordinary job and make it ten times more complex than originally intended. Frankly, I don't see it that way. There are always extenuating circumstances. You have to be flexible. If you discover something that will improve the plan, it seems within reason to adopt it. How you plant a few flowers depends on your definition of *plant*. My definition just happens to be a bit more involved than most. I want things done right: according to *my* standards, not my husband's.

Fortunately, my husband had left the truck, so I could get some manure to add to the soil. He had already put some in, but I didn't think it would be enough, so I added more. That made the flower bed mound up too high, which didn't fit my landscaping plan.

After contemplating what was at hand that I could use for a short retaining wall, I remembered a magazine photo of a woodsy flower garden held back by wrist-size logs. We had an old pile of logs. I began wheelbarrowing the wood to my intended flower patch.

After lunch, I dug a trench and placed each log on end, side by side, so it would look rustic but orderly. Finally, after securing the posts with our heavy clay soil, I stepped back to admire my work. The logs stuck up too high. Rather than pull them out and lower them, I figured it would be easier to add more dirt to the planter. The wheelbarrow and I headed for some great soil elsewhere on our three-acre property.

By now my planter had grown to 5 feet by 7 feet and 18 inches high. The six pansies looked anemic by themselves. I scrounged through other beds to find extra flowers or shrubs to fill in the bare areas. I moved four columbines and two calla lilies, some scotch moss, and a small fern. It wasn't enough. But that small fern gave me an idea. Several varieties of fern grow down by our creek. I seized my shovel and headed down the hillside.

Three trips later, with sore muscles, scratches from battling blackberries, and mud all over me, I emerged with the last large fern. By 4 that afternoon I had finished planting the flower bed. It looked fantastic.

"And how long did this take you?" my husband growled.

"Oh, I puttered at it most of the day. Doesn't it look great?"

"It looks wonderful, but I'm sure you did too much."

"I'm fine. Just a little tired."

Funny how God waits until you are most receptive to hear Him. The next morning, every movement redefined pain for me. It even hurt to just lie there. *If only I had listened to my husband, this wouldn't have happened.*

A DIFFERENT DEFINITION

That was a surprising first thought, because listening to my husband and doing what he says are two different things, based on my definition of submission: yielding when it is convenient. *None of that Ephesians 5:22 wimpiness for me! I can take care of myself quite well, thank you. I certainly don't need a man to tell me what to do, considering the stupid mistakes men make. Marriage is a 50-50 deal: Both have input. When we don't agree, we argue until I win. It's that simple.*

That Sunday at church, our pastor addressed marriage and the perfect relationship between Adam and Eve.

Here we go again, I thought. *Another "Submit and be trampled on" lecture.*

"He created them so their abilities, personalities, gifts, and bodies complemented each other," our pastor said. "Together, they were complete. They made all their important decisions together—look at Genesis 1:28: 'God blessed them and said to them . . . fill the earth and subdue it. Rule over . . . every living creature.'"

This was news to me. Adam and Eve were to rule *together?* I thought it was all Adam's job. But what if they didn't agree? Then what?

Before the Fall, Adam and Eve focused on God and each other. But when sin entered in, they became self-absorbed. The consequences of sin corroded their relationship. They threw out God's standards of what was best for them and adopted their own.

Had I created my own standards, too?

THE WORLD'S STANDARDS

It made me wonder how much of the world's view I have bought into—thinking I'm superwoman and can ignore my doctor's directions, my husband's leading, my God's commands. . . .

God declared His curses, and put the man over the woman "He will rule over you" (Gen. 3:16). Not a happy moment for any of us. My husband and I struggle over domination. Even when I win, I'm not content. Certain passages in Scripture are difficult to read because I do not want to obey them.

I am an intelligent woman: I supervise a messy household, discern what I don't need to buy from telephone solicitors, quickly perceive when a bad decision is about to be made, and use good judgment to correct it. To me, *submission* means I lose my identity, my choices, my control. It conjures up images of passivity, resignation, surrender. The dictionary confirms it. The only snag? God's dictionary differs from ours.

STUDYING THE BIBLE

If I thought my pansy lesson bad, what happened next only made it worse. A friend called to ask if I had any material on Proverbs 31—the "perfect wife." *Oh please! I don't want to go there.* Why she thought I'd have that kind of information escapes me. But two days didn't pass and another friend called to ask the same question. *What is this, a conspiracy?* When a third woman, in her 70s, called the same week to tell me she was mentoring a young woman and wanted to know if I could give her some direction, I got the feeling that God wanted me to take a look for myself. Grudgingly, I did.

Hebrew writers generally summarized the entire passage at the end, so I skipped the "ugly stuff" and immediately read the last verses: If a woman feared the Lord, she deserved to be praised. *That's fine, but what about all that spinning and sewing stuff? And her lamp not going out at night?* My sewing would attract jeers, not cheers. And I can't be prepared for everything.

I began looking for answers in the church library. Perhaps something had been written about the culture of the times that would explain this workaholic superwoman. It took more than one book, but I learned some fascinating things that changed my perspective.

Sewing and spinning were considered menial tasks, usually done by the poor or by slaves. No woman of means (like the woman described in Proverbs 31) would do such a lowly chore. Her lamp was the visual reminder of God's leading, carried over from the Exodus. Maybe our interpretation has been, "Be prepared," but to her it symbolized God's presence in the home.

As I discovered the cultural background, I thought, *what kind of woman would do the work of a slave? Or give the slave girls scarlet overgarments when the standard practice was to provide just the white undergarment? A humble woman, a generous woman. A caring woman.* Her lamp did not go out at night. She was a woman who looked to the Lord, first, and responded to others out of the character God had developed in her.

This woman did not strike me as subservient! Her husband "has full confidence in her," and "is respected at the city gate." Hmmm. *Could this mean that he didn't worry about what she might do when he wasn't there? Could the same be said for me?* I thought about my empty promise to my husband about planting those pansies. Whoops.

RECONSIDERING EPHESIANS

I returned to Ephesians again, but with a different attitude. In the past, I had read 5:22 out of context, so I looked at the whole book. The first part speaks about the body of Christ, how each one of us has been given gifts to use for the body, and how the body works together in unity to build each other up in love (Eph. 4:1–16). Paul then goes on in chapter 5 to encourage us to understand what the Lord's will is, to "Submit to one another out of reverence for Christ" (v. 21).

1 saw the next verse in a whole new light. "Wives, submit to your husbands as to the Lord. For the husband is the head of the wife as Christ is the head of the church" (v. 22–23). Would I tell Christ not to worry about what I was doing that day? I don't think so. Especially when I knew I had a plan for those pansies that I had not completely revealed. This is not just about submitting to my husband; it's about submitting to Christ.

SPOUSES NEED EACH OTHER

Women need men to call us up toward the highest moral principles; they need us to call them down to the warmth of human love and respect for gentler sensibilities (which includes keeping dirty socks out of the den). And just as domesticity and fidelity are not *imposed* on men by women—in marriage as God intended it, that commitment is a potential that was just waiting to be realized—so rigorous justice is not a purely male construction to which women must submit.

Frederica Mathewes-Green, *Christianity Today*, November 17, 1997.

As I began to put together the picture in Ephesians of what a husband/wife relationship is supposed to look like, it reminded me of Adam and Eve ruling together. They were not concerned with themselves, but built each other up in love, encouraged each other to grow in their relationship with God. They would listen to the other's concerns and opinions—and when an agreement could not be reached, Eve would willingly yield her desires. She did not do this because Adam was smarter, or bigger, or because he was the man. She yielded to him because that glorified God.

Our culture, propelled by women's organizations, glorifies women. Yet women still lack what they want from men: respect. In our effort to gain their respect, we fight for equivalent pay, contest the glass ceiling, and demand to be recognized as equals. But we sometimes look down on men, almost with disdain. Do we want to be equal, or do we want to be better?

For a woman to yield to a man is tantamount to treason in today's society. Yet it is what God requires of us. By being submissive, we can win over our husbands who are not obeying God's Word, without saying a thing. It will be our character they notice, and that is what is pleasing to God (1 Peter 3:1–4).

This isn't easy to hear, or to implement. When my will says, "I want it my way!" the last thing I want to do is to let my husband have the final word. What if he's wrong? What if our security is destroyed by his decision? What if we lose the house? What if we end up living on the streets? What if it was my decision that caused those things?

Yes, men are accountable, too. Paul reminds husbands to love their wives . . . to cherish them (Eph. 5:25). Peter instructs men to live considerately, giving honor to the woman (1 Peter 3:7). What woman would not love that to happen in her marriage? But when I manipulate my husband by Scripture to convict him of his sin, I lessen the Holy Spirit's importance, and feed my pride in my knowledge of what God says. My responsibility is to be obedient to God first.

AN AMAZING OUTCOME

An interesting thing happened when I decided to submit, to willingly yield control to my husband: I began to respect him more. He began to ask my opinion. I stopped trying to lead the family, and he began to lead. It didn't happen right away. It took a lot of squirming in my chair while I waited for him to act, and a lot of discussion with God about my attitude.

I also wanted to show respect to my husband, so I looked for things he did that I appreciated. Then I told him. At first, it seemed so phony. "I really appreciate your faithfulness in providing for our family." "Thanks so much for taking out the trash. I appreciate it." "Thanks for helping me pick up this mess before everyone arrived." Each time I would praise him on something, it got easier. *Please* and *thank you* were heard in our home more often. I discovered things he did that I had never noticed before.

No, not everything is wonderful. I find myself fuming at times, biting my tongue when it's obvious he's making a stupid decision! But I made a commitment to the Lord first, and it requires me to sacrifice my desires once in a while. But isn't that what God requires of us anyway? To sacrifice our desires so He can be seen and glorified? I do find overall I am much happier, more content than in the past. I also find myself on my knees before God almost daily for my husband. If he has the final decision, I want God's help for him as much as possible so he makes the right one!

Now that I am trying to obey God in our marriage, I've observed other women who are working on the same thing. Interestingly, most of them are involved at our church in various aspects of leadership, as are their husbands. Their demeanor as a couple attracts others to them. Couples who struggle with their relationship are encouraged by those in obedience, but I wonder if they recognize what is truly going on in those homes. Submission is such a despised concept.

I never thought I would support that ugly "S" word. I wish I could change the world's definition of it. But at least I changed mine. Today I worked in the garden, and I didn't keep it a secret from my husband. I like to think of it as my sacrifice to God.

| "The doctrine that women should 'submit graciously,' taken to an extreme, can lead to abuse."

MARRIAGES WILL NOT IMPROVE IF WIVES SUBMIT TO THEIR HUSBANDS

Cokie and Steven Roberts

In the following viewpoint, Cokie and Steven Roberts contend that the Southern Baptist resolution declaring women should submit to their husbands is misguided and is not the best way to improve marriage. According to the Roberts, the Baptist view does not acknowledge that gender equality has become more common in marriage. In addition, they argue, wifely submission could increase the problem of spousal abuse. The Roberts assert that marriage needs to be encouraged and supported but not under the Southern Baptist model. Cokie Roberts is a political news reporter and Steven Roberts is the Shapiro Professor of Media and Public Affairs at George Washington University in the District of Columbia.

As you read, consider the following questions:

1. Why do the Roberts agree that men should provide for and protect their families?
2. According to statistics cited by the authors, what proportion of households consists of married couples with children?
3. What are the benefits of marriage, according to the authors?

Reprinted from Cokie and Steven Roberts, "The Baptist Family: A Distorted Outlook," *Dallas Morning News*, June 19, 1998, by permission of United Feature Syndicate, Inc.

The good news: Traditional families are making a comeback.
The bad news: The Southern Baptists have a deeply distorted view of what those families are or should be.

At their 1998 convention in Salt Lake City, the Baptists adopted a resolution saying a man has a "God-given responsibility to provide for, to protect and to lead his family." A wife should "submit graciously to the servant leadership of her husband."

We endorse the provide and protect part. Too many men don't take responsibility for their families, and if anything, there should be stronger laws against deadbeat parents who avoid child support edicts.

MALE SUPREMACY DOES NOT MAKE SENSE

But we have a lot of trouble with the Baptists' idea of leadership. With more and more women out in the work force, living the same lives and earning the same salaries as their husbands, the whole notion that gender determines supremacy in a marriage makes less and less sense. Not that it ever did.

A few years ago, while we were returning from abroad, Steve found himself staring at the little white card handed out by immigration officials. It asked for our "head of household."

Steve realized the question didn't apply. For years, we had done exactly the same job—reporting about Congress and politics. At times, we have made different salaries, but all decisions, about finances or anything else, always have been shared equally. Our household has two heads. Or none. But not one.

The Baptists' statement not only is inaccurate in many cases, it also is potentially dangerous. The doctrine that women should "submit graciously," taken to an extreme, can lead to abuse, both physical and emotional. This country has come a long way in terms of making spousal abuse illegal, and the last thing women need is a church sanctifying the notion that their "God-given" role is submission to men.

Let us be clear: We are ardently pro-family. Almost 32 years of marriage demonstrate our commitment to that institution.

MARRIAGE IS MAKING A COMEBACK

Sure, marriage isn't for everyone. Some folks are happier staying single, and others feel liberated when they finally flee a bad union.

But it is our experience that most adults are better off coupled, and after decades of disaster, matrimony is making a comeback. Not a big one, but the trend is encouraging.

In 1970, married couples with children accounted for two

out of five households. Twenty years later, that number had plunged to only one out of four. Since 1990, the rate has held steady. The decline has stopped.

A few years ago, the Census Bureau was predicting that five out of 10 new marriages would fail. That is down to four out of 10.

Sociologists say it has to do with aging baby boomers, who now are more settled and less restless, but our experience suggests another possible explanation. Young people getting married today look at the let-it-all-hang-out, do-your-own-thing generation and say, "That isn't for me. That isn't the way I want to live."

Wasserman ©1998, Boston Globe. Distributed by Los Angeles Times Syndicate. Reprinted with permission.

Steve was stunned in 1997 when he showed his writing class at George Washington University a column about our daughter's wedding. Several young women said, "I can't relate to that scene, your daughter has two parents still married to each other, my parents are divorced, and the whole idea of a wedding scares me."

Now, some of those young people might decide not to get married at all. But we think the more common reaction is this: When I get married, I won't make the mistakes my parents made. I won't saddle my kids with all the stress and guilt they dumped on me.

Marriages Provide Hope

Even in June, not all marriages are made in heaven. But most of them are, and it is good news for all of us that more of them now are expected to survive.

Part of the benefit is financial: Intact families are far less likely to wind up on welfare. But the deeper reason is less tangible. We all are blessed by a new marriage, by its sense of hopefulness and conviction and sacrifice.

That is why marriage is such a communal event. And that is why we were pleased recently when, in the middle of a wedding, the minister asked the congregation to pledge their support to the young couple.

They will need it. So will all of us.

So we all are for marriages, new and old. Just not for the model outlined by the Southern Baptists.

"We seem to be in the process as a
society of redefining our marriage
culture with a new emphasis on
mutuality."

MUTUAL RESPECT BETWEEN SPOUSES
WILL IMPROVE MARRIAGE

Don Browning

In the following viewpoint, Don Browning maintains that marital love based on mutuality—the notion that people should give their spouses and children the respect and affection they expect for themselves—may represent the best model for marriage in the future. He contrasts mutuality with self-sacrifice and self-fulfillment, options that focus on the needs of only one of the spouses. According to Browning, the mutuality approach could help end the divorce culture and improve marriage. Browning is an Alexander Campbell professor of ethics and the social sciences at the University of Chicago Divinity School.

As you read, consider the following questions:

1. What percentage of Americans say that marital love is best defined by mutuality, as cited by the author?
2. According to statistics cited by Browning, what percentage of women favor mutuality?
3. In Browning's view, how does the Promise Keepers movement appear to support mutuality?

Reprinted from Don Browning, "Self-Sacrifice, Self-Fulfillment, and Mutuality: The Evolution of Marriage," The Responsive Community, Winter 1997/1998, by permission of The Responsive Community.

Our intensifying national debate about marriage and the "divorce culture" is also, at least implicitly, a debate about models of marital love. Do we have a right to demand that marital love yield a high degree of personal fulfillment? And do spouses, as a corollary, have a right to terminate a marriage that fails to produce such personal satisfaction? Or is such an expectation inimical to stable marriages? Should young people rather be taught that marital love entails continual self-sacrifice? The divorce culture is often blamed on the prevalence of the personal fulfillment emphasis, while some of the most powerful reactions against the divorce culture—the Promise Keepers movement is an example—seem to fall back on the traditional, self-sacrifice theme.

MARITAL LOVE IS CHANGING

Based on an opinion survey, one thing seems clear: couples today perceive themselves as practicing a style of marital love quite different from that of their parents. While contemporary couples tend to see their parents as having emphasized *self-sacrifice* in marital love, most describe themselves as practicing a form of marital love that puts a greater emphasis on *mutuality*. Whether this perceived shift from self-sacrifice to mutuality bodes good or ill for marriage remains unclear. What is clear is that today's couples see themselves as approaching marital love in a different spirit from that of the past.

For our book, *From Culture Wars to Common Ground: Religion and the American Family Debate*, my co-authors and I—Bonnie Miller McLemore, Pamela Couture, Bernie Lyon, and Robert Franklin —surveyed 1,019 Americans in cooperation with the George H. Gallup International Institute. These men and women were asked about their marriages and how they defined love in a successful marriage. We gave them three different definitions of love to choose from: (1) the *self-sacrifice* option (love "means putting the needs and goals of your spouse and children ahead of your own"); (2) the *self-fulfillment* model (love "fulfills your personal needs and life goals"); and (3) the *mutuality* standard (love "means giving your spouse and children the same respect, affection, and help as you expect from them").

A clear majority (55 percent) of Americans said that love in a good marriage is best characterized by mutuality. But, as can be seen in the table, our respondents perceived their parents as having approached marriage differently. When asked to characterize their mothers' and fathers' approach to marriage, less than 30 percent said their parents would have selected mutuality as the preferred style. Fifty-six percent thought their mothers would have selected self-sacrifice; 40 percent thought their fathers would have selected self-sacrifice, while 28 percent thought their fathers would have selected self-fulfillment.

MODELS OF LOVE			
		Beliefs of	
Model of Love	Respondent	Mother*	Father*
Mutuality	55%	29%	28%
Self-Sacrifice	38%	56%	40%
Self-Fulfillment	5%	9%	28%

*That is, respondent's perception of what would have been his or her mother's and father's beliefs

CONFLICT, COHABITATION, RELIGION, AND GENDER

One may note that very few (5 percent) of our respondents chose the "self-fulfillment" option as best. But when people were asked which model of love they followed when in an actual conflict with an intimate partner, 13 percent chose the more individualistic view of love while only 45 percent chose mutuality and 28 percent self-sacrifice. People acknowledge, as one might expect, that in the heat of conflict they are more self-regarding than when considering relationships in the abstract.

There was one revealing exception to the overall pattern of the survey. Cohabiting, nonmarried respondents were far more inclined than married respondents to choose the self-fulfillment option, and far less inclined toward the self-sacrifice choice. Fifty-two percent of cohabiting individuals believed a good relationship correlates with mutuality, but only 17 percent believed self-sacrifice is important, while fully 21 percent were willing to say that love as self-fulfillment is best.

Overall scores in the survey varied somewhat according to age, education, income, marital status, religious experience, political convictions, and race. The young were slightly more inclined to emphasize mutuality and self-fulfillment than self-sacrifice. The more highly educated were also higher on mutuality.

There was also a somewhat predictable difference in emphasis between mainline and evangelical Protestant respondents. In situations of conflict with intimates, religious liberals were high on mutuality. Sixty-one percent of Episcopalians and 49 percent of Presbyterians (both mainline denominations) elected mutuality. Only 13 percent of Episcopalians elected self-sacrifice as did only 18 percent of Presbyterians. On the other hand, Southern Baptists (the largest evangelical denomination) were less likely to choose mutuality and more likely to choose self-sacrifice than either religious liberals or the population as a whole. Thirty-nine percent of Southern Baptists preferred self-sacrifice in the heat of conflict, in contrast to 28 percent for the population as a whole.

Finally, women were significantly more likely than men to define ideal marital love in terms of mutuality and significantly less likely to opt for self-sacrifice. Sixty-one percent of women chose mutuality, in comparison to only 48 percent of men. Conversely, 44 percent of males linked self-sacrifice with a good marriage while only 33 percent of females made that connection. Among African-Americans, the gender gap was even more pronounced. Seventy-six percent of black women opted for mutuality, in contrast to a mere 33 percent of black men. Only 14 percent of black women saw self-sacrifice as ideal, in contrast with 48 percent of black men.

SELF-SACRIFICE MAY NO LONGER WORK

What generalizations can we make about this data? While our data says nothing about how an earlier generation actually saw marriage, it does seem to show that today we perceive our model of marriage as changing—couples see themselves as emphasizing mutuality to a far greater degree than their parents did. To be sure, the preference for mutuality remains a function of gender (with women gravitating more to this definition than men), of income and education (with higher income and education individuals favoring mutuality more), and of political-religious orientation (mutuality is more popular among members of liberal, mainline religious denominations than among members of conservative evangelical ones).

Yet the growing consensus around mutuality suggests that efforts to beat back the divorce culture through a simple reassertion of older ideas of self-sacrifice may not meet with success in contemporary society. On the contrary, we seem to be in the process as a society of redefining our marriage culture with a new emphasis on mutuality. Although there is surely a place for self-sacrifice in marital love, it is best to conceive it as the extra effort needed to restore a relationship to mutuality.

The Promise Keepers movement might seem to represent an important exception to this trend. Their leadership stresses both traditional self-sacrifice and the role of the husband as the "spiritual leader" of the family—ideas that might seem to part ways with the contemporary emphasis on mutuality. Significantly, however, nine out of ten attendees surveyed at the Promise Keepers October 1997 Washington rally told pollsters from the *Washington Post* that "husbands and wives should 'share equally' in doing the housework, disciplining the children, and 'making the big decisions.'" So even the members of this culturally conservative movement appear not unaffected by the move toward mutuality in the larger marriage culture. (This is true in spite of the persistent tendency of some leaders of Promise Keepers to designate men as the family member charged with the responsibility of making final decisions about what constitutes mutuality and fairness.)

The primary lesson is that our marriage culture is evolving— something that in our policy discussion and cultural debate we need to acknowledge. The task of overcoming the divorce culture and building a more healthy marriage culture should not simply attempt to turn back the clock on our ideas of marriage, but rather should build constructively on the ideal of mutuality that has become so central to our contemporary understanding of the marriage bond.

"Many men realise that the images of masculinity they grew up with do not work."

MEN NEED TO DEVELOP A NEW MASCULINITY

Paul Lashmar

In the following viewpoint, Paul Lashmar asserts that the war between the sexes has left men at a crisis point and that, in order to improve their situation, men must redevelop the notion of masculinity. He claims that men need to find a way to define themselves that does not rely on power and status but rather focuses on their emotions and energy. In addition, Lashmar argues that men and women need to cease the sex war and work together to better the lives of both genders. Lashmar is a television producer and journalist.

As you read, consider the following questions:

1. Why does Lashmar believe men are in retreat in the war between the sexes?
2. In the author's view, who benefited most from the feminism of the 1960s?
3. What is Lashmar's view on androgyny?

Reprinted from Paul Lashmar, "The Men's Gloom (Feminism and Men)," *New Statesman & Society*, March 8, 1996, with permission; © The Guardian, London.

"**M**en are the enemy. They know it—at least they know there is a sex war on, an unusually cold one." It is now several decades since Germaine Greer wrote those words. Is it time to call a ceasefire in the sex war or at least enter into a constructive dialogue?

THE GENDER WAR CONTINUES

The causes of this uncivil war were clear enough, and for three decades the battle for equality has, often out of necessity, been hostile and divisive. But events are overtaking us that require co-operation rather than conflict. The gender debate has become too remote from the great economic and political shifts of the past 17 years. The 1990s are a desperate age of unemployment, broken homes, overworked mothers, absent fathers, physical and sexual abuse, lack of community, declining spirituality, glamorised violence, and, most of all, the dysfunctional criminalised energy of many young men.

All around us relationships that should exist don't, those that do disintegrate, often from enormous external pressure, while the current nuances in the gender debate have little or no impact on most people's lives. What is desperately needed, in therapist Susie Orbach's phrase, is "emotional literacy", but most of us remain illiterate. This needs action at both the personal and the wider political level.

Are men still the enemy? Author Marilyn French says: "Women cannot distinguish which men are enemies and which are not." That is a profoundly depressing statement. It offers men no way forward. It also denies the men that take responsibility. The war continues unabated.

In the 30-year war, men are in retreat. By the year 2000 there will be more women in employment than men. Women are performing better academically. There still remain substantial issues of inequality for women, not least in pay, but a great deal of progress has been made. The roles of women and men are undergoing the greatest changes in history. In her 1990 book, *The Demographic Revolution*, Jane McLaughlin wrote: "One of the anthropological pleasures of the 1990s will be watching how men cope with a new role—the redundant male." And so it has come to pass.

MASCULINITY NEEDS TO CHANGE

Men are in crisis. In less than a generation, many of the key roles by which masculinity has been traditionally judged have either become redundant or men are increasingly excluded—

the breadwinner, the craftsman, the father, the husband and the soldier.

It is understandable that a certain schadenfreude can be felt at seeing men being routed. But should men be totally dispossessed? I talked with a redundant miner in Grimethorpe [a town in England]. He was unable to find work and was suffering from clinical depression. His wife had three part-time jobs to make ends meet. He found childcare difficult and had lost his sense of manhood. Neither of them liked this abrupt reversal of the status quo.

Men need to find a new way of masculinity that does not depend on external status and is emotionally satisfying not only to them, but to their partners as well. It must not be based on power and control. Men need to work together to do this—it is their responsibility. And they seek a masculinity that is not a denial of the male, but optimises the positive and creative energies of men.

In the wake of feminism, many men realise that the images of masculinity they grew up with do not work. As Vic Seidler, a writer on men's issues, says: "If we live in a 'man's world' it is not a world that has been built on the needs and nourishment of men. Rather it is a social world of power and subordination in which men have been forced to compete if we want to benefit from our inherited masculinity."

FACING THE ISSUES

All over [Great Britain] men are now working in different ways on these problems. It has surprised me, in men's groups I have attended, how much pain men carry. Anger at the father leaving during childhood. Inability to conduct good relationships. Hurt from physical and sometimes sexual abuse from relatives. Feelings of inadequacy from childhood bullying. Devastation by the loss of a family after divorce. There are endless permutations. Men must find their pain, look it in the eye, own it and deal with it.

The sex war has achieved much for women, but the feminism of the 1960s has benefited middle-class women most of all. It is they who are most likely to achieve career, relationship and children. Thus, in many middle-class households there are two working parents, often backed up by nannies and other part-time domestics. Yet in many working-class households neither partner can find work or it maybe the woman who has to go out to several "McJobs".

In that rarified part of society where the gender debates take place, sometimes referred to as "the chattering classes", a surprising honesty has begun to emerge. Neither men nor women can sustain the omnipotent images of the "Master of the Universe" or "Superwoman" for long. There has been a spate of articles that suggest we all might just be human after all, have our limitations and need the help of a wider community.

ANDROGYNY IS NOT THE ANSWER

In the 1990s, feminism has diverted into some intriguing but ultimately esoteric issues. On Radio 4 [a British radio station], Shere Hite was selecting some of her favourite prose. She chose a poem on androgyny. In her introduction, Hite extolled androgyny as the future, as though imprecise sexuality would be the answer to gender conflict. This is a popular line of thought. For some people it might be true. But for most it is as realistic as the 1960s assumption that race problems would be solved "by having coffee-coloured people by the score".

Most people want to have a viable heterosexual relationship and possibly children. While gender is partly a social and cultural construct, most people believe there are core differences in masculine and feminine. Yet they hear nothing that helps them to find ways of tackling the confusion and uncertainty in their lives.

REJECTING A CAPITALIST VIEW OF MASCULINITY

A radical change in the dominant culture of masculinity [is necessary], such that men no longer feel compelled to stake their self-worth on earnings, job prestige, and power in the workplace. The mythopoetic men recognized that these measures of a man's worth caused problems. They also tried to resist this culture of masculinity by valuing men's abilities to imagine, to love, to nurture, to feel, and to respond aesthetically and spiritually to the large and small wonders of life. In this way, too, the mythopoetic movement marked a progressive break from the soulless culture of capitalism. Perhaps the mythopoetic critique of traditional masculinity will inspire more men to question what they have taken to be the goals of a worthy life and to reject the poisonous criteria of self-worth that a capitalist culture instills in us.

Michael Schwalbe, *Unlocking the Iron Cage: The Men's Movement, Gender Politics, and American Culture*, 1996.

The first attempt at all-party talks in the sex war was the "Women and Men: working together for a change" conference in June 1996. It was organised by people from a diverse range of backgrounds including *Human Potential* magazine, Wild Dance

Events, *Achilles' Heel* magazine, Women's Communication Centre, Neal's Yard Agency for Personal Development, *London Spark* magazine, psychotherapy, business, media and the arts.

One of the conference speakers, therapist Andrew Samuels, has pointed out that men are still in the driving seat when it comes to power, "but if the linkage could be made between the emotional realities of male vulnerability and the social and economic inequality (of women), then we could begin to think in terms of a partnership or alliance between women and men." I hope so.

"*A sexual contract reconstructed around the idea of men as the main family providers is the best overall model.*"

A RETURN TO SOME TRADITIONAL GENDER ROLES WOULD IMPROVE SOCIETY

Geoff Dench

Returning to some traditional gender roles, such as allowing men to be the primary economic providers, would better society, argues Geoff Dench in the following viewpoint. He asserts men cannot become more civilized unless they feel responsible for the well-being of others; therefore, Dench argues, women should not seek full equality in the marketplace because that will marginalize men. Dench maintains that women should instead return to their role as moral trustee within the private domain. Dench is the author of *Transforming Men: Changing Patterns of Dependency and Dominance in Gender Relations*, the book from which this viewpoint is taken.

As you read, consider the following questions:

1. According to Dench, what is the basis for hostility toward voluntarily single mothers?
2. Why does Dench think that many women have been unwilling to admit their desire for men to retain the breadwinner role?
3. What happens when women seek freedom, in the author's opinion?

If the emphasis on equality were less strict, or it were replaced by an idea of sexual equity which recognized the continuing importance of zones of priority, so that men's work still figured as a crucial contribution, I think that there would be no problem with allowing women much more scope in the market than they have enjoyed in the past. The prospect of full equality is however a serious demotivator of men, and does not I believe even correspond to what most women want. By its nature it is not likely to be objectively achieved to the satisfaction of its advocates until much of the male workforce has effectively lost heart and run away. So the sooner it can be replaced by a more ambiguous and less challenging goal, the better for us all.

Women do in any case need to remind each other that the private domain will decay unless enough of their energy is given to it, and they re-invest it again as the palace at the centre of civilized life. This realm is much more than homemaking and domestic drudgery, as it includes numerous moral trustee roles in the local community and society as a whole, which men know that they can never perform equally because of their greater distance from the sources of community values and reciprocity. A significant part of this trustee role consists in helping to transform a man or men into responsible providers, and this is surely the root of traditional hostility to voluntarily single mothers, which feminists affect to find so incomprehensible.

ALTERNATIVE FAMILIES CAN EXIST

There seems to be no imperative to go "back" to old ideas about compulsive monogamy and captive homemakers. In those societies where most families are now having few children there is room for a lot of flexibility, provided that enough positions of main breadwinning, as a basis of fathering, are available for most men who need it. If women genuinely want it, we can surely together envisage a range of co-existent alternative models. For example, there seems no compelling reason why a woman who wants children by different men should not, as among the Nuer, create several fractional male providers instead of one; and men for their part can collect fractions. If this helps to finish off the concept of men as heads of household, then so be it. The age of vaudeville is long gone and in contemporary circumstances it would be more appropriate to portray sexual partnerships as entailing equal levels of responsibility in different realms. Within this broad division of labor it would seem reasonable that where women are particularly devoted to their careers they should be seen as justified in throwing themselves mainly into the public realm and perhaps hiring other people to do most of their private domain work for them, or even, arguably, combining with kindred spirits to run female joint-households in which domestic chores are shared between full equals. [Author and sociologist] Charles Murray can envisage a wide range of options:

> This doesn't mean that a mother must marry. If a single woman making £50,000 a year wants to have a baby and continue her career while paying for professional child care, that's her business. If a less affluent woman knows she can count on support from her parents, fine. If the local feminist support group is willing to provide her with a stipend to raise the child, fine. I am not recommending that the state forbid single women from choosing to have babies. It should simply stop subsidising that choice.

That menu could be extended considerably as perhaps by, in the spirit of workfare, the idea that the state might offer some support by organizing grouped or shared accommodation for single mothers, so enabling them to pool some child care and make themselves more available for other work in the public realm.

Any resulting shortfall of father-provider roles is not likely to be very great so long as the bottom line governing all of these options is that women should look first to interpersonal relations rather than to generalized patriarchs-as-taxpayers for their lines of material support, and are willing to go along with a presumption that men have slightly greater moral entitlement to paid jobs than they do, and to a higher rate of remuneration as a "family wage." Women are not going to be locked up in kitchens. However, what they should not expect is equal rights in the market.

WOMEN DO NOT WANT FULL EQUALITY

I do not believe that most women want fully equal rights with men in the public realm. They want to take part in the world outside of domesticity; but they also want men to go on playing the breadwinner role which they recognize as the male route to finding family and community commitment. But many have been afraid to come out with this in case feminists attack them for weakness and sororal betrayal. There is a great gulf between activists and the bulk of women who just want some modest and practical improvements in their lives, and most of the renegades mocked or vilified by [feminist and author] Susan Faludi were offering variations on this point. It was, for example, the main theme of Sylvia Ann Hewlett's book *Lesser Lives*, which Faludi savages for presenting "merely anecdotal" evidence that ordinary women were not seeking full economic equality.

But Faludi's own case that equal opportunity militants reveal the true soul of women is itself only tenuously supported by the complex evidence which she parades. During her final rallying call to the troops to go out and claim their birthright, she suggests that by vigorously challenging the conventional definition of masculinity, women can allow men (thanks, Sue) to start questioning it, too.

> After all, to a great extent so many men have clung to sole-provider status as their proof of manhood because so many women have expected it of them. (In the Yankelovich poll, it's not just men who have consistently identified the breadwinner role as the leading masculine trait; it has also consistently been women's first choice.)

What she seems to be letting out here, perhaps unwittingly, is that women do want and "expect" men to be providers; and the exhortation to challenge conventional definitions is actually aimed by her towards women. Thus, after 494 pages (in a main text of 498) of thundering variations on the theme that men are conspiring to force women back into the kitchen, the placards finally slip to reveal that after a full generation of feminist propaganda most women don't actually want to compete with men at work after all—certainly not once they have children. Moreover the wording in this poll refers to "sole-providing," which is more strongly exclusive of women than the main providing which most men would settle for. What more evidence could any of us ask for?

Most women, if allowed to speak freely, would agree that a sexual contract reconstructed around the idea of men as the

---

FEMINISTS HAVE DENIGRATED TRADITIONAL ROLES

Engrossed in pursuits without purpose, feminists have eschewed the traditional supportive role, which sustained man at a far higher level of performance than would otherwise have been possible; and which converted the symbolic strut of youth into a meaningful, generation spanning, commitment to family. But in this process of transforming our upward momentum into a living for the moment self-indulgence, they have failed to demonstrate any unique ability in the new worldly yet artificial lifestyle—or anything with long-term social value comparable in any way to the excellence once demonstrated by their female ancestors. . . . The whole approach has denigrated the roles of wife and mother, for which their sex alone has been equipped by nature—and which must remain always, their one clear area of marked superiority.

Jacob van Flossen, *Return of the Gods*, 1998.

---

main family providers is the best overall model available as it seems to generate the greatest sum total of inputs to community life. It does not allow most women as much freedom from interpersonal obligations as men enjoy, but this sort of symmetry of destiny is not feasible. If women go for freedom, men just take even more for themselves. The best way to get their help is to give them the status and position which will prompt them to relinquish more of their natural freedom. Broadly speaking a woman's life combines security and independence most effectively within the framework of a conjugal system in which men's membership of and standing within a community hang on their performance as dutiful partners and fathers. That is what she has had in mind throughout history when drawing up sexual contracts.

WOMEN NEED TO MAKE SACRIFICES

Some sacrifices by women are entailed in this. But reciprocity always requires that, and if women don't sacrifice themselves a bit then they will not be able to ask men to do the same. The nature of society is such that chains of sacrifice originate with, and are initiated by, women. This is what makes society possible. While it may arise out of biological roles, it is in itself a moral and spiritual phenomenon, and cannot be reduced to them. It is not, in the jargon, an essentialist proposition. (And even if it is, then so be it.)

Over-emphasis on female independence, and rejection of sacrifice, has spawned a frog culture in which the sexes are polarizing, and men are becoming increasingly marginal as they revert to a wild state. Their objective social inferiority is potentially much greater than any secondary public status assigned to women under patriarchy, and lacks the compensation of a countervailing domain to sustain them. Is that really what women want? Not many, I think. Women want men to be responsible people like themselves. But few will be if women deny them reasonable opportunity to acquire what most people need in order to become civilized beings, and that is personal dependents—other people for whom to be responsible.

On that basis men are capable of becoming much better partners than may seem possible just at present. This is how women throughout history have transformed them into useful members of communities. I suspect that it will be by making refinements within this general system, not by any radical abandonment of sexual divisions of labor altogether, that women will carry forward the process of social evolution.

PERIODICAL BIBLIOGRAPHY

The following articles have been selected to supplement the diverse views presented in this chapter. Addresses are provided for periodicals not indexed in the *Readers' Guide to Periodical Literature*, the *Alternative Press Index*, the *Social Sciences Index*, or the *Index to Legal Periodicals and Books*.

Betty Carter and Joan K. Peters	"Remaking Marriage & Family," *Ms.*, November/December 1996.
Charles S. Clark	"Marriage and Divorce," *CQ Researcher*, May 10, 1996. Available from 1414 22nd St. NW, Washington, DC 20037.
Scott Coltrane	"Families and Gender Equity," *National Forum*, Spring 1997. Available from the Honor Society of Phi Kappa Phi, Box 16000, Louisiana State University, Baton Rouge, LA 70893.
Danielle Crittenden	"Q: Is Early Marriage the Best Choice for American Women? Yes: By Marrying Young, Women Will Be Happier as Wives, Mothers and Employees," *Insight*, February 22, 1999. Available from 3600 New York Ave. NE, Washington, DC 20002.
Jon Davies and Norman Dennis	"From the Tyranny of Rules to the Whim of Relationships: The Family in Modern Society," *World & I*, December 1995. Available from 3600 New York Ave. NE, Washington, DC 20002.
Jean Bethke Elshtain	"The Future of the Family?" *World & I*, December 1995.
Kay S. Hymowitz	"Where Has Our Love Gone?" *Wall Street Journal*, April 6, 1995.
Christopher B. Jones	"Women of the Future: Alternative Scenarios," *Futurist*, May/June 1996.
Frederica Mathewes-Green	"Men Behaving Justly," *Christianity Today*, November 17, 1997.
Gustav Niebuhr	"Southern Baptists Declare Wife Should 'Submit' to Her Husband," *New York Times*, June 10, 1998.
Jennifer L. Pozner	"Q: Is Early Marriage the Best Choice for American Women? No: This One-Size-Fits-All Prescription Ignores Individual Goals, Dreams and Pocketbooks," *Insight*, February 22, 1999.

Katie Roiphe   "The Independent Woman (and Other Lies),"
                        Esquire, February 1997.

Anita Taylor   "Women and Men Communicating: Who's
                        from Mars?" *Vital Speeches of the Day*, February
                        15, 1999.

Barbara Dafoe   "Women and the Future of Fatherhood,"
Whitehead   *Wilson Quarterly*, Spring 1996.

A.N. Wilson   "The Good Book of Few Answers," *New York
                        Times*, June 16, 1998.

FOR FURTHER DISCUSSION

CHAPTER 1

1. The authors in this chapter discuss the influence of biology and culture in determining male/female differences. Which influences, if any, do you think are strongest? Explain your answer, drawing from the viewpoints and personal observations.

2. John Leo contends sexual quotas in jobs are wrong because men and women have different skills due to their brain structure. Do you agree with him? Why or why not?

3. Chuck Colson and Alex Gino disagree on the effectiveness of surgery for children born of indeterminate gender. Whose argument do you find more convincing and why?

CHAPTER 2

1. The authors in this chapter debate the roles of women in modern society and whether women still face discrimination. Do you think that women's roles are improving? What steps, if any, are needed to better the status of women in today's world? Explain your answers, drawing from the viewpoints and any relevant personal experiences.

2. Lawrence W. Reed and Katha Pollitt disagree over the accuracy of the publication "Women's Figures," citing different statistics to support their views on discrimination against women in the workplace. Whose use of statistics do you find more convincing? Do you think gender discrimination in the workplace is a problem? Explain your answers, drawing from the articles and any personal observations.

3. Marian Kester Coombs and Joan Smith disagree on how society views motherhood and women who choose not to be mothers. Do you think society is destroying or overexalting motherhood? Why or why not?

CHAPTER 3

1. According to Allan G. Johnson, the media does not accurately report on the problem of male violence toward women. R.F. Doyle contends that the media ignores men's issues and concerns. Based on these readings, do you think that the media truthfully depicts men's roles? Explain your answer.

2. Waller R. Newell asserts that male aggression toward women has been due to thirty years of social engineering. Do you agree with his thesis that men are not naturally inclined toward violence against women? Why or why not?

3. Stephen Chapman argues that the marginalized role of fathers and husbands in modern society is detrimental to women and their children. Olga Silverstein and Beth Rashbaum contend that, while fathers can be beneficial, they are not required for a child to thrive. Whose argument do you find more convincing and why?

Chapter 4

1. Christine McClelland uses passages from the Bible to support her view that women should submit to their husbands. Do you think these passages accurately reflect the conditions of modern marriage? Why or why not?
2. Geoff Dench maintains that certain traditional gender roles must be retained in order to improve society. In your opinion, is this a viable solution? Do you think that gender roles do need to change in the future and if so, in what ways? Explain your answers.

ORGANIZATIONS TO CONTACT

The editors have compiled the following list of organizations concerned with the issues debated in this book. The descriptions are derived from materials provided by the organizations. All have publications or information available for interested readers. The list was compiled on the date of publication of the present volume; the information provided here may change. Be aware that many organizations take several weeks or longer to respond to inquiries, so allow as much time as possible.

Center for the American Woman and Politics (CAWP)
Eagleton Institute of Politics, Rutgers University
New Brunswick, NJ 08901
(732) 932-9384 • fax: (732) 932-6778
e-mail: gmm@rci.rutgers.edu
website: http://www.rci.rutgers.edu/~cawp/

CAWP is a think tank and resource center dedicated to the advancement of women in public leadership. The center offers public leadership programs for women, research on the importance of electing women to all levels of government, and current information on the women's political movement. Many of its published materials, including *Political Women Tell What It Takes* and *Women Make a Difference*, are available through its website.

Center for the Study of Popular Culture (CSPC)
9911 W. Pico Blvd., Suite 1290, Los Angeles, CA 90035
(310) 843-3699 • fax: (310) 843-3692
e-mail: info@cspc.org • website: http://www.cspc.org

CSPC is a conservative educational and legal-assistance organization addressing such topics as political correctness, feminism, and discrimination. The Individual Rights Foundation, the legal arm of the center, is devoted to establishing gender-neutral standards in public life. The center publishes books, pamphlets, and the magazines *FrontPage* and *Heterodoxy*.

Eagle Forum
PO Box 618, Alton, IL 62002
(618) 462-5415 • fax: (618) 462-8909
e-mail: eagle@eagleforum.com • website: http://www.eagleforum.org

Eagle Forum is an educational and political organization that advocates traditional family values. To expose what it perceives as radical feminism's goal to break up the family, the forum examines and disseminates its position on issues such as women in combat, family leave, childcare, tax credits for families with children, and "outcome-based" education. The organization offers several books and publishes the monthly newsletter *The Phyllis Schlafly Report*.

Families and Work Institute (FWI)
330 Seventh Ave., New York, NY 10001
(212) 465-2044 • fax: (212) 465-8637
website: http://www.familiesandwork.org

The Families and Work Institute is a nonprofit organization that addresses the changing nature of work and family life. It is committed to finding research-based strategies that foster mutually supportive connections among workplaces, families, and communities. More than forty research reports are available for sale from the Institute, including *The 1997 National Study of the Changing Workforce, Ahead of the Curve: Why America's Leading Employers Are Addressing the Needs of New and Expectant Parents,* and *Working Fathers: New Strategies for Balancing Work and Family.*

The Howard Center
934 North Main St., Rockford, IL 61103
(815) 964-5819 • fax: (815) 965-1826
e-mail: Howard@profam.org • website: http://www.profam.org

The Howard Center works to return America to Judeo-Christian values and supports traditional families and gender roles for men and women. It studies the evolution of the family and the effects of divorce on society. The center offers three monthly publications: *The Family in America, The Religion & Society Report,* and *New Research.*

Independent Women's Forum (IWF)
PO Box 3058, Arlington, VA 22203-0058
(800) 224-6000 • (703) 558-4991 • fax: (703) 558-4994
e-mail: info@iwf.org • website: http://www.iwf.org

The Independent Women's Forum is a nonprofit, nonpartisan organization founded by women to foster public education and debate about legal, social, and economic policies affecting women and families. The IWF is committed to policies that promote individual responsibility, limited government, and economic opportunity. It publishes *The Women's Quarterly* journal.

Men's Defense Association
17854 Lyons St., Forest Lake, MN 55025
fax: (651) 464-7887
e-mail: info@mensdefense.org • website: http://www.mensdefense.org

The association promotes equal rights for men and gathers research, compiles statistics, and offers an attorney referral service for male victims of sex discrimination. It publishes the newsmagazine the *Liberator* and the pamphlet *The Men's Manifesto.*

Mothers at Home (MAH)
8310A Old Courthouse Rd., Vienna, VA 22182
(800) 783-4666 • (703) 827-5903 • fax: (703) 790-8587
e-mail: MAH@netrail.net • website: http://www.mah.org

Mothers at Home is a national organization that strives to enable women to stay at home and take care of their children rather than enter the workforce. Its members oppose the view that every woman should have a job and a career. MAH helps women become at-home mothers by offering them support, education, and networking, and it provides the public with education and public policy analysis. It publishes several books as well as the monthly journal *Welcome Home*.

National Center for Fathering

PO Box 413888, Kansas City, MO 64141-3888
(913) 384-4661 • fax: (913) 384-4665
e-mail: dads@fathers.com • website: http://www.fathers.com

The National Center for Fathering is a nonprofit research and education organization which seeks to champion the role of responsible fatherhood by inspiring and equipping men to be more engaged in the lives of children. The Center is a resource for men seeking to strengthen their fathering skills. It publishes a wide variety of books about fathering and the quarterly newsletter *Today's Father*.

National Coalition of Free Men (NCFM)

PO Box 129, Manhasset, NY 11030
(516) 482-6378
e-mail: ncfm@ncfm.org • website: http://www.ncfm.org

The coalition is a nonprofit educational organization whose mission is to examine men's lives, with particular emphasis on how sex discrimination affects men. In order to raise public consciousness about little-known topics dealing with the male experience, the coalition conducts research, sponsors educational programs, and provides speakers. Its newsletter, *Transitions: Journal of Men's Perspectives*, is published bi-monthly and offers statistics, book reviews, movie reviews, and events affecting men.

National Men's Resource Center

PO Box 800, San Anselmo, CA 94979
e-mail: help@menstuff.org • website: http://www.menstuff.org

The National Men's Resource Center is an on-line nonprofit educational organization dedicated to fostering positive change in male roles and relationships. It offers resources covering all six major segments of the men's movement (men's rights, mythopoetic, pro-feminist, recovery, re-evaluation counseling, and religious) with information on over 100 men's issues. Its website contains information, resources, a calendar of men's events, and an extensive list of publications, including *Silent Sons: A Book For and About Men* and *Proving Manhood: Reflections on Men & Sexism*.

National Organization for Women (NOW)

1000 16th St. NW, Suite 700, Washington, DC 20036
phone: (202) 331-0066 • fax: (202) 785-8576
e-mail: now@now.org • website: http://www.now.org

The National Organization for Women is a grassroots lobbying organization with over 500 chapters nationwide. Through education, protests, and litigation, it supports equal rights for women, equal pay for women workers, and affirmative action. NOW advocates equality for military servicewomen and favors allowing women to serve in combat roles. The organization publishes the *National NOW Times.*

National Partnership for Women and Families
1875 Connecticut Ave. NW, Suite 710, Washington, DC 20009
(202) 986-2600 • fax: (202) 986-2539
website: http://www.nationalpartnership.org

The National Partnership for Women and Families is a nonprofit, non-partisan organization that uses public education and advocacy to promote fairness in the workplace, quality health care, and policies that help men and women meet the demands of work and family. Its monthly newsletter, reports, and press releases are available for viewing on its website.

9to5 National Association of Working Women
231 W. Wisconsin Ave., Suite 900, Milwaukee, WI 53203
(800) 522-0925 • (414) 274-0925 • fax: (414) 272-2970

The organization seeks to gain better pay, opportunities for advancement, elimination of sex and race discrimination, and improved working conditions for female office workers. It publishes the *9to5 Newsletter* five times a year as well as numerous pamphlets.

Status of Women Canada (SWC)
360 Albert St., 7th Fl., Ottawa, Ontario K1A 1C3 CANADA
(613) 995-7835 • fax: (613) 957-3359
e-mail: webcoord@swc-cfc.gc.ca • website: http://www.swc-cfc.gc.ca

Status of Women Canada is a federal government agency which promotes gender equality and the full participation of women in the economic, social, cultural, and political life of the country. SWC publishes the quarterly newsletter, *Perspectives,* and numerous reports, including "Economic Gender Equality Indicators" and "Round Table Report on the Portrayal of Young Women in the Media."

Wider Opportunities for Women (WOW)
815 15th St. NW, Washington, DC 20005
(202) 638-3143 • fax: (202) 638-4885
e-mail: info@w-o-w.org • website: http://www.w-o-w.org

WOW works to expand employment opportunities for women by overcoming sex-stereotypic education and training, work segregation, and discrimination in employment practices and wages. In addition to pamphlets and fact sheets, WOW publishes the book *A More Promising Future: Strategies to Improve the Workplace* and the quarterly newsletter, *Women at Work.*

Women Work! The National Network for Women's Employment
1625 K St. NW, Suite 300, Washington, DC 20006
(202) 467-6346 • fax: (202) 467-5366
e-mail: womenwork@womenwork.org
website: http://www.womenwork.org

Women Work! fosters the development of programs and services that prepare women for the workforce. It acts as a clearinghouse, providing the public with technical assistance, training, information, data collection, legislative monitoring, and other services. It also provides referrals and information on research in progress and available programs. Women Work! develops and publishes a range of materials including program curricula, legislative guides, statistical reports and the quarterly newsletter *Network News*.

BIBLIOGRAPHY OF BOOKS

Ken Abraham	*Who Are the Promise Keepers?: Understanding the Christian Men's Movement.* New York: Doubleday, 1997.
David Blankenhorn	*Fatherless America: Confronting Our Most Urgent Social Problem.* New York: BasicBooks, 1995.
Deborah Blum	*Sex on the Brain: The Biological Differences Between Men and Women.* New York: Viking, 1997.
Phyllis Burke	*Gender Shock: Exploding the Myths of Male and Female.* New York: Anchor Books, 1996.
Elinor Burkett	*The Right Women: A Journey Through the Heart of Conservative America.* New York: Scribner, 1998.
Pat Califia	*Sex Changes: The Politics of Transgenderism.* San Francisco: Cleis Press, 1997.
Phyllis Chesler	*Letters to a Young Feminist.* New York: Four Walls Eight Windows, 1997.
Ellis Cose	*A Man's World: How Real Is Male Privilege—and How High Is Its Price?* New York: HarperCollins, 1995.
Danielle Crittenden	*What Our Mothers Didn't Tell Us: Why Happiness Eludes the Modern Woman.* New York: Simon & Schuster, 1999.
Geoff Dench	*Transforming Men: Changing Patterns of Dependency and Dominance in Gender Relations.* New Brunswick, NJ: Transaction Publishers, 1996.
Alice Domurat Dreger	*Hermaphrodites and the Medical Invention of Sex.* Cambridge, MA: Harvard University Press, 1998.
Nigel Edley and Margaret Wetherell	*Men in Perspective: Practice, Power and Identity.* London: Prentice Hall/Harvester Wheatsheaf, 1995.
Margrit Eichler	*Family Shifts: Families, Policies, and Gender Equality.* Toronto: Oxford University Press, 1997.
Richard Ekins	*Male Femaling: A Grounded Theory Approach to Cross-Dressing and Sex-Changing.* London: Routledge, 1997.
Diane Eyer	*Motherguilt: How Our Culture Blames Mothers for What's Wrong with Society.* New York: Times Books/Random House, 1996.
Barbara Findlen, ed.	*Listen Up: Voices From the Next Feminist Generation.* Seattle: Seal Press, 1995.
Elizabeth Fox-Genovese	*Feminism Is Not the Story of My Life: How Today's Feminist Elite Has Lost Touch with the Real Concerns of Women.* New York: Nan A. Talese, 1996.

Linda Bird Francke

Ground Zero: The Gender Wars in the Military. New York: Simon & Schuster, 1997.

Betty Friedan and
Brigid O'Farrell, ed.

Beyond Gender: The New Politics of Work and Family. Washington, DC: Woodrow Wilson Center Press, 1997.

F. Carolyn Graglia

Domestic Tranquility: A Brief Against Feminism. Dallas: Spence, 1998.

Germaine Greer

The Whole Woman. New York: Knopf, 1999.

Michael Gurian

A Fine Young Man: What Parents, Mentors, and Educators Can Do to Shape Adolescent Boys into Exceptional Men. New York: Jeremy P. Tarcher/Putnam, 1998.

Anita M. Harris

Broken Patterns: Professional Women and the Quest for a New Feminine Identity. Detroit: Wayne State University Press, 1995.

Bernice L. Hausman

Changing Sex: Transsexualism, Technology, and the Idea of Gender. Durham, NC: Duke University Press, 1995.

Sharon Hays

The Cultural Contradictions of Motherhood. New Haven, CT: Yale University Press, 1996.

Clinton J. Jesser

Fierce and Tender Men: Sociological Aspects of the Men's Movement. Westport, CT: Praeger, 1996.

Allan G. Johnson

The Gender Knot: Unraveling Our Patriarchal Legacy. Philadelphia: Temple University Press, 1997.

Meredith M. Kimball

Feminist Visions of Gender Similarities and Differences. Binghamton, NY: Haworth Press, 1995.

Michael Kimmel

Manhood in America: A Cultural History. New York: Free Press, 1996.

Molly Ladd-Taylor and
Lauri Umansky, eds.

"Bad" Mothers: The Politics of Blame in Twentieth-Century America. New York: New York University Press, 1998.

Ralph LaRossa

The Modernization of Fatherhood: A Social and Political History. Chicago: University of Chicago Press, 1997.

Karen Lehrman

The Lipstick Proviso: Women, Sex & Power in the Real World. New York: Doubleday, 1997.

Ronald F. Levant and
William S. Pollack, eds.

A New Psychology of Men. New York: Basic Books, 1995.

James A. Levine and
Todd L. Pittinsky

Working Fathers: New Strategies for Balancing Work and Family. Reading, MA: Addison-Wesley, 1997.

Nan Bauer Maglin
and Donna Perry, eds.

"Bad Girls"/"Good Girls": Women, Sex, and Power in the Nineties. New Brunswick, NJ: Rutgers University Press, 1996.

Rhona Mahony — *Kidding Ourselves: Breadwinning, Babies, and Bargaining Power.* New York: Basic Books, 1995.

Meredith Maran — *Notes from an Incomplete Revolution: Real Life Since Feminism.* New York: Bantam Books, 1997.

Brian Mitchell — *Women in the Military: Flirting with Disaster.* Washington, DC: Regnery, 1998.

George L. Mosse — *The Image of Man: The Creation of Modern Masculinity.* New York: Oxford University Press, 1996.

Cornelius F. Murphy Jr. — *Beyond Feminism: Toward a Dialogue on Difference.* Washington, DC: Catholic University of America Press, 1995.

Robert Nadeau — *S/he Brain: Science, Sexual Politics, and the Myths of Feminism.* Westport, CT: Praeger, 1996.

William S. Pollack — *Real Boys: Rescuing Our Sons from the Myths of Boyhood.* New York: Random House, 1998.

David Popenoe — *Life Without Father: Compelling New Evidence That Fatherhood and Marriage Are Indispensable for the Good of Children and Society.* New York: Martin Kessler Books, 1996.

Deborah L. Rhode — *Speaking of Sex: The Denial of Gender Inequality.* Cambridge, MA: Harvard University Press, 1997.

Anne Richardson Roiphe — *Fruitful: A Real Mother in the Modern World.* Boston: Houghton Mifflin, 1996.

Michael Schwalbe — *Unlocking the Iron Cage: The Men's Movement, Gender Politics, and American Culture.* New York: Oxford University Press, 1996.

Pepper Schwartz and Virginia Rutter — *The Gender of Sexuality.* Thousand Oaks, CA: Pine Forge Press, 1998.

Wendy Shalit — *A Return to Modesty: Discovering the Lost Virtue.* New York: Free Press, 1999.

Howard Sieberman — *Exposing Feminism: How Feminist Concepts Hurt America.* Boston: Branden, 1999.

Robert S. Sigel — *Ambition and Accommodation: How Women View Gender Relations.* Chicago: University of Chicago Press, 1996.

Joan Smith — *Different for Girls: How Culture Creates Women.* London: Chatto & Windus, 1997.

Paul Smith, ed. — *Boys: Masculinities in Contemporary Culture.* Boulder, CO: Westview Press, 1996.

Frederick Sontag — *The Descent of Women.* St. Paul, MN: Paragon House, 1997.

| Judith Stacey | *In the Name of the Family: Rethinking Family Values in the Postmodern Age*. Boston: Beacon Press, 1996. |

| Lauri Umansky | *Motherhood Reconceived: Feminism and the Legacies of the Sixties*. New York: New York University Press, 1996. |

| Susan Walzer | *Thinking About the Baby: Gender and Transitions into Parenthood*. Philadelphia: Temple University Press, 1998. |

| Stephen Wicks | *Warriors and Wildmen: Men, Masculinity, and Gender*. Westport, CT: Bergin & Garvey, 1996. |

| Riki Anne Wilchins | *Read My Lips: Sexual Subversion and the End of Gender*. Ithaca, NY: Firebrand Books, 1997. |

INDEX